Swing Trading Strategies for Beginners: 3-Hour Crash Course

Learn Stocks and Options to Build Passive Income From Home

Edward Day

from various sources. Please consult a licensed professional before attempting any techniques outlined in this book.

By reading this document, the reader agrees that under no circumstances is the author responsible for any losses, direct or indirect, that are incurred as a result of the use of the information contained within this document, including, but not limited to, errors, omissions, or inaccuracies.

Table of Contents

Introduction

"There is a time to go long, a time to go short and a time to go fishing" - Jesse Livermore

Have you ever tried to trade the markets before? If your answer is yes, then you're not alone. Pretty much everyone tries to make money trading at some point in their lives. Here's another question: Have you been successful at it?

The number of people that answer in the affirmative to this question are far fewer in number. In fact, according to research carried out by the news outlet DailyFX, almost 90% of traders end up losing their capital within a year of opening their accounts (Rodriguez, 2017).

Such numbers tend to intimidate beginners. More often than not, the average unsuccessful trader has tried implementing buy and hold strategies with varying degrees of success in the past. Buy and hold is an extremely long-term oriented strategy and there's no telling when your investments will pay off.

Trading, on the other hand, is a far more active pursuit. It involves working in the markets intimately, and tends to offer far more insights into human behavior. While buy and hold seeks to insulate the investor from human emotions, trading strategies, such as the ones you'll be learning in this book, seek to take advantage of them.

Greed and fear are ever present in the markets, and I'll be teaching you how you can take advantage of these emotions by flipping them within your head. Before we get to all of that, there are many other things you need to learn. Most importantly, you need to understand that buy and hold investing calls for a very different approach than the one you will need when swing trading.

Short Versus Long Term

My objective with this book is to help you understand the benefits of short term swing trading. It isn't to tell you that buy and hold investing is bad. In fact, as you read this book, you'll figure out that many of the methods you use to screen long-term stock investment strategies can be used to identify short-term plays as well.

Correlated assets are a good example of this. Correlation refers to the relationship between two asset classes. For example, gold has always been viewed as a hedge or a safety net whenever the United States is in turmoil or if it's suffering from a financial crisis.

By spotting movements in certain asset classes, you can take advantage of movements in other assets as well.

This is just one method you'll be learning in this book. I will be focusing on technical analysis as well, since trading without this is a bit like trying to win a 100 m race while hopping on one leg.

The most important part of your trading education is risk management. Far too many traders invest their time in learning how markets work from a technical perspective. However, learning your technical strategy is one thing, but learning to make it work for you over the long term as the market changes is entirely another.

This is what risk management boils down to. It helps you keep the money you've earned over the long run, and stops you from making silly mistakes that cause traders to lose money. Your mindset is a part of risk management and you'll be learning all about this in the later chapters of this book.

Understanding your mindset involves figuring out how greed and fear dominate our minds when we're trading in the market. The successful trader isn't someone who has overcome these emotions. Instead, they're someone who's learned to think about the markets correctly. Learn how to think correctly, and you'll find that you won't need to control your emotions or be fearful of your mind being clouded by them.

As a part of helping you fulfill your trading dreams, I've also outlined a simple seven-step process that will help you understand all the steps involved in becoming a successful trader. Some of these steps will take time while you will breeze through others with ease.

The key is for you to focus on executing these steps instead of worrying about how 'soon' you'll get there. Remove time from the equation right now. I'm saying this because it's a mistake that I made myself when I first started trading.

Who am I?

My sole trading journey officially began in 2008, but truth be told, the seeds were planted well before this. I was born in New York City and earned a Bachelor's degree in Accounting, followed by a master's degree in the same subject. I worked as a chartered accountant for a reputed firm and enjoyed a stable career.

I enjoyed my work, but there was always something nagging me, it felt as if I wasn't fulfilling my potential. I valued the stability my job brought to my life, but knew there had to be more to life than just seeking stability. As if on cue, I received an opportunity through one of my clients.

He was a full-time forex trader, and I was curious about how he made money for a living. He invited me to a seminar, and I was immediately hooked. He was kind enough to mentor me during my earlier stages of learning, but it wasn't long before I discovered that I had a built-in instinct for the markets.

I signed up for all the forex courses I could lay my hands on and began working towards my Bachelor's degree in Economics as well. I was thirsty for knowledge and my hunger for trading mastery was insatiable!

By 2008, I was ready to leave accountancy behind and dove full-time into my forex trading activities. These days, I live in Chicago with my wife and two daughters. I love fishing and walking our two dogs. Aside from trading, I also regularly participate in forex trading seminars in my area as a speaker.

I mentor students that approach me since I believe it's important to give back in some way what I received when I was learning the art of trading. While I can safely say that I have mastered the art of trading, my passion lies in sharing my knowledge and learning even more about the markets.

Don't be intimidated by reading about my current situation. Instead, focus on the fact that I started out like everyone else; I didn't have any huge internal advantages when beginning. This book is my attempt to give you what my mentor originally gave me, valuable guidance and pointers on how to build the life of your dreams.

Trading is a great way of doing this and the freedom you will receive is unparalleled. However, you'll need to work for it. There are no shortcuts! Do the work as prescribed in this book and you'll find that success and money are easily achievable.

Take the time to study the chapter on risk management, along with the chapters on trends and ranges, it is the most important part of this book. You're going to be learning a ton of new concepts here so take your time to understand everything.

Are you excited yet? Let's get started!

Chapter 1:

The Basics of the Market

In order to learn how to trade, you'll need to first understand where you'll be trading. Jumping into technical analysis, without taking the time to understand how the market works, is a lot like trying to drive without understanding what the brake pedal does or where the engine is in your vehicle.

Unsuccessful traders will usually skip this step entirely due to greed motivating them. They're so keen on making money that they forget to learn how to go about making it! You're going to be successful, so obviously, you're going to avoid making that mistake.

Some of the material in this chapter might be known to you. I still encourage you to read through it. You might learn something new that you've missed before. The best place to begin is to really understand what a financial market is. Much like a market for produce or for cars, a financial market is a place where buyers and sellers of financial instruments interact with one another.

All financial markets can be classified into one of the following categories:

1. Stock
2. Bond
3. Derivatives
4. Forex

These categories divide the markets on the basis of the financial instruments that are traded within them. Stock markets are where shares of companies are bought and sold. Bond markets are where bonds of organizations are bought and sold. Derivatives are traded in both stock and bond markets. Lastly, forex markets are where currency pairs are traded.

You'll often hear the term OTC being used in relation to the markets. This stands for Over the Counter. OTC markets are thinly traded and don't have too many traders present in them. This means the instruments offered within them are subject to huge levels of risk.

Bond derivative markets are traded OTC. Typically, the large investment banks of the world are the ones that trade them among each other. This means every single instrument's price depends on what a handful of traders think it's worth. What increases risk levels is that these instruments are usually worth over $100 million each!

It takes a lot of skill to trade such markets and this is why the average trader is not allowed access to them. This brings us to the way in which traders themselves are classified. There are two categories that apply here: Retail and Institutional.

Anyone with an account size that is less than seven figures is considered a retail trader. Such traders have access to many brokerage houses but don't have access to so-called prime brokers. Prime brokers offer a larger variety of exotic financial instruments to trade.

They cater exclusively to institutional clients. Despite the seven figure threshold, the larger Wall Street banks consider anyone with less than a billion dollars in capital to be small.

Many traders feel that institutions have an edge over retail traders. In some ways this is true. However, there are many advantages that the retail trader has, it all comes down to what sort of a game you want to play. The market is great because everyone has to play in the same playground. There isn't a different league or stage that institutional traders have to operate in compared to retail traders.

Technically bond derivative markets operate as a separate space, but you don't need to trade those markets to make money. Think of the market as an ecosystem. Everyone is connected to one another. If you can carve out a little niche for yourself within the market, you'll be extremely successful. You don't have to defeat the large traders or even play the games that they do.

This is why the market offers so many wonderful opportunities for everyone. Your background or IQ doesn't matter. All that matters is whether you're willing to do the work that is necessary to be successful. As long as you do this, you'll make a lot of money. So let go of any fear you might have of institutional traders. The strategies in this book will keep you away from them and for the most part, you won't even know they exist.

Coming back to the topic of markets, there are two further ways in which they can be classified, centralized and decentralized. Centralized markets are what you hear about most of the time, this is what the stock exchanges are.

Exchanges

Have you heard of the New York Stock Exchange? What about the National Association of Securities Dealers Automated Quotations (NASDAQ)? Odds are you must have heard of them if you've ever switched on the financial news or even read a blog post. These are examples of stock exchanges.

Stock exchanges are private companies that make their money by charging transaction fees for every trade that is placed through them. There are big exchanges like the NYSE and NASDAQ, and then there are smaller ones such as Investors' Exchange (IEX), Better Alternative Trading System (BATS), NYSE Arca, and so on.

There are also private stock exchanges called dark pools that are operated by prime brokers for their large clients. For example, if Warren Buffett wants to buy stock in a company, he's not doing it on the NYSE. He communicates his order to Goldman Sachs, and they buy it for him through a pseudonym in a dark pool.

The one factor that is common throughout all of these exchanges is that all of them have a centralized order book. The order book is an electronic record of who's traded what. If you buy a single share of WMT (Walmart) through your broker, this goes into the order book record.

The presence of an order book creates a certain type of market environment. You might be scandalized by this, but stock exchanges regularly sell their order books to the higher bidder. Over the past decade, High Frequency Trading or HFT firms have become more prominent. The most famous of these firms is Citadel corp. This is a secretive hedge fund that wield enormous clout over the exchanges.

They happen to be the biggest source of fees for them and, as a result, stock exchanges tend to service their accounts on a priority basis. Companies such as Citadel use the order book to figure out which stock is experiencing high volumes and practice a trading method called front running.

If WMT is experiencing high demand, HFT firms can detect this and place orders nanoseconds before the high volume hits. They buy all available WMT stock and resell it for a fraction of a profit. All of this is done through algorithms which explains the speed. While the per trade profit is extremely low, by placing billions worth of orders every day, they manage to turn those fractions into millions in profit everyday.

As a retail trader this means you will see markets behave in odd ways when you place your orders at extremely obvious levels or close to them. The markets will move close to them and either miss the level or hit the level and go back the other way. There are ways to mitigate this and I'll be discussing it when talking about placing stop loss orders later in this book.

Despite the heavy presence of algorithms, you should not be afraid of them, or think that the markets are rigged; it's simply a factor you're going to have to deal with. Instead of worrying, learn how to adapt. This is how good traders behave and you can't fight it, so instead, figure out what works and practice that.

When trading you won't be placing orders directly with an exchange since you will need to be of an institutional size to do this. You will be placing orders through an intermediary such as a broker. I'll discuss brokers in detail in the next chapter.

Stock exchanges allow you to trade the following financial instruments:

- Stocks
- Futures
- Options

Let's now move on and look at decentralized markets.

Decentralized Markets

If centralized markets are characterized by the presence of an order book, decentralized markets are just the opposite, they don't have one. That sounds simple enough to understand! An OTC market is an example of a decentralized market. These markets function as a network of dealers.

For example, when bond derivatives are traded, a dealer at Goldman Sachs gets on the phone with someone at JP Morgan Chase and negotiates a price. The person at JP Morgan might have heard something about this instrument from someone at Morgan Stanley that may or may not be true.

Either way, the lack of an order book doesn't mean that participants are unaware of what's happening with other traders in the market. It's just that there is no definitive data to rely on since these transactions aren't being recorded anywhere.

The biggest OTC, or decentralized market that exists, is the Forex or FX market. FX is a $5.1 trillion one (Segal, 2017). Its size is larger than all the world's stock markets combined. The market functions as a network with all the dealers in it being the large investment banks of the world.

Each investment bank serves as a liquidity provider or LP to a number of smaller brokers who, in turn, serve customers such as you. Every bank specializes in certain currencies. For example, Goldman Sachs isn't the place to go if you want to buy large quantities of Japanese Yen.

You wouldn't approach Nomura or MUFG to buy the Australian Dollar (Aussie). In other words, every dealer has good knowledge of what's going on with their own currency, but has a less than perfect view of what others are doing. The large number of banks within the dealer network also makes it tough to accurately gauge trading volumes.

Of course, it is possible to make judgements on the basis of macroeconomic forecasts, but this can be hit or miss. What makes things a bit more complex is that the FX market doesn't trade currencies by themselves. Instead, pairs of currencies are traded.

Currency Pairs

Here is an example of a currency pair: EURUSD. This pair contains two currencies, the Euro and the US Dollar. The EUR is called the base currency, and the USD is the quote currency. If you see a price for EURUSD as being equal to 1.2345 this means one Euro (base) is worth 1.2345 (quote) USD.

Currency pairs exist between all the freely traded currencies in the world. The Chinese Renminbi is not freely traded, and you're not going to be able to speculate on its relationship with other currencies in the world. However, the currencies of all major economic zones, such as the Eurozone, the United Kingdom, the USA, Japan, Australia, New Zealand and Switzerland are freely available for you to trade.

The currency pairs that form between all of them and the U.S. Dollar are called the major pairs. Pairs formed between these currencies among themselves are called the minor pairs. Despite the term, there is nothing minor about them. All of them are freely traded and there are many traders available to trade with. Because of this, you're not going to face any price shocks as there is always someone wanting to trade them.

Given that the prices of these currency pairs are just the exchange rates between them, it stands to reason that they won't move too much. After all, you cannot expect the Euro to be worth two USD today and three tomorrow. Such movement would cause gargantuan economic crises!

The moves within the FX market are measured in terms of pips. A pip is 0.0001, which is the equivalent of one hundredth of a cent in pairs that involve the Dollar, and is used in the case of all currency pairs except the Yen. In the Yen's case it is 0.01. A move of 50-100 pips is considered huge, which translates to around a cent or slightly less than that.

If the moves are so small, how is a trader supposed to earn a profit?

Leverage

This is where leverage comes into the picture; it allows you to borrow money from your broker and trade with it. Here's a simple example of how leverage boosts your returns. Let's say you buy something worth $100 but place just $1 on it, and borrow the rest to finance this trade, and then the stock moves by just one percent to $101. While the overall trade has earned one percent, your cash on cash return is 100% because your cash investment in the trade is just one dollar. A movement of one dollar in the overall price nets you a 100% gain before you pay interest on your leverage.

This is how it works in forex as well. FX instrument sizes are called lots. A single lot contains 100,000 of the base currency. If you buy a lot of EURUSD, you've just bought 100,000 Euros. This is an astronomical amount of money. However, you don't have to put up all of this amount as cash. Instead, you use leverage. In the United States, brokers provide a maximum leverage of

1:50, so you can borrow $50 for every dollar you invest. In this case, you can buy 100,000 Euros by placing 2,000 Euros upfront with your broker (or the Dollar equivalent of 2,000 Euros).

If this is also too large an amount, you can buy a mini lot. A mini lot is 10,000 of the base currency. This reduces your investment to 200 Euros. If even this amount is too much, you can buy a micro lot which is 1,000 of the base currency.

Some brokers quote lot sizes while others quote an abbreviation. A standard lot of 100,000 is abbreviated to '1' while a mini lot of 10,000 is reduced to 0.1. A micro lot of 1,000 is reduced to 0.01. You can buy a position that is depicted as 2.12. This means you're buying two standard lots, one mini lot and two micro lots. There are some brokers that offer so-called nano lots as well, which are 100 units of the base currency. This doesn't make a huge difference to your trading since almost everyone will have the trading capital to cover at least a mini lot.

Calculating Profit and Loss

Calculating profit and loss in forex is not as straightforward as it is with stocks. With stocks, you're dealing with just one currency. All you need to do is subtract your buying price from your selling price and multiply that by the number of shares (units) you've bought, and that's your profit.

With FX, you need to convert values between currencies. The easiest and least time-consuming way of doing this is to use online calculators. Use the one at babypips.com and you'll be just fine. I would go so far as to say that you don't even need to understand the specifics of the calculation. Your broker will do this automatically for you.

Market Hours

Something that differentiates the FX market from stock markets is that the former don't close at the end of the day. They are global markets and run 24 hours a day, five days a week. The market officially opens when the time is 8 A.M. in Auckland, New Zealand, but throughout the day, volumes will rise and fall depending on which financial center is online.

The Asian session is the earliest of the 24-hour day with Tokyo, Sydney and Hong Kong dominating trading volumes. Next comes the European session that is dominated by London. The first two hours of the London session overlaps with the final two of the Asian session.

The final four hours of the London session overlaps with the first four hours of the New York or American session. This is the most heavily traded part of the forex day. As London goes offline, volumes decrease, and as New York closes, minor centers such as Dallas and San Francisco take the lead. However, volumes are abysmal during these times. The market meanders on until Auckland reopens the next day, which is around midnight in New York.

Major currency pairs are heavily traded throughout the day until the New York closes. The 'close' here refers to when the market in New York shuts. Minor currency pair volumes depend on whether their home markets are online. For example, the AUDJPY, which is the Aussie Dollar and Japanese Yen, is most active during the Asian session. Its trading volume drops once the session ends. Pairs such as the CADJPY, the Canadian Dollar and the Yen, see volumes during the Asian session and in the New York session as well.

Swaps

Another phenomenon that exists in forex that is missing in stocks, is that of swap rates or carry rates. When you trade a currency pair, you're simultaneously buying one currency and shorting the other. For example, if you buy 1.2 EURUSD, you're buying 1.2 Euros and shorting 1.2 USD. Since you're shorting USD, your broker will borrow this amount for you and you'll have to pay interest on this. However, since you've bought EUR, you get to earn interest on this as well. This means your cost of carrying the position is the interest paid on the USD subtracted from the interest earned on the EUR.

This is called the swap or carry rate. If you own a currency that has a high-interest rate (as defined by its central bank) and sell a currency with a low-interest rate, you will earn positive carry. You'll be paid to own that position.

The carry trade used to be an extremely profitable strategy in the early 2000s, thanks to the interest rate differential between the Japanese Yen and the U.S. Dollar. With the Yen's rates close to zero, the Alan Greenspan led Fed set high rates for the dollar, so going long on the USDJPY was an extremely profitable trade.

In most cases, the carry paid overnight was more than enough to overcome any losses in the position. These days carry opportunities exist in thinly traded currency pairs and are risky to place. However, in the future there might be opportunities to place such a trade.

Options

Leaving behind the world of FX, we return to the stock market. Specifically, you're now going to learn about the derivatives market that exists with the stock market. A derivative is a financial instrument that derives its value from another. An options contract is an example of a derivative.

There are two kinds of options that will be available to you as a retail trade: calls and puts. Options contracts have what is called an underlying instrument, in the stock market, the underlying is stock of a company. Every options contract covers 100 shares of the underlying.

Call options give you the right to buy the underlying at a certain price (Kuepper, 2020). This price is called the strike price. Puts give you the right to sell the underlying at a certain price. This contract is valid for a month and has an expiry date.

Let's understand this through an example. Walmart stock (WMT) is currently trading for $123.96. You'll find there are options available for different expiry dates. It's a good idea to look at options that are expiring at least 30 days or more from the current date. This allows you to fully capture all the gains they promise.

If you think that the stock price is going to increase to at least $140 within a month, you can buy the 130 call option. You'll pay $1.11 for this (called the premium) and it gives you the right to buy WMT at $130 should the price of the underlying rise above this. If it rises to $140, you can exercise your option and buy WMT for $130, resell it for $140 and earn a $10 profit per share.

Your profit will be $10 minus the premium you paid to buy the option. Similarly, with a put, if the price decreases below the strike price by the expiry date, you can exercise the put, sell the underlying and cover your short by buying it back for the lower underlying market price.

Alternatively, you could simply trade the options themselves. Options premiums fluctuate depending on how close or far away the underlying is from the strike price. I must mention that options lend themselves to numerous strategies, thanks to the way they're structured.

In this book, I'm not going to cover options specific strategies. Instead, you can use the strategies and tools in here to swing trade options.

Here are a few tips that will help you do this effectively:

1. Always purchase options that are at least 30 days away from expiry. This allows you to experience a decent swing in prices, and it also gives you room to allow the underlying to move as well.

2. Despite the 30 days expiry, you don't need to hold on to your options contract for that long. You can exit your position before the expiry date.

3. Do not short options. Instead, buy the opposite type of contract. If you think the underlying is going to fall in price, don't short a call. Buy a put instead. To successfully short options, you need to understand options specific strategies, and these are a completely different way of trading. As such, they aren't swing trades.

4. You can speculate in options that are close to expiry. However, these will be more volatile. Trade options that are far from expiry before getting closer.

5. Understand the implications of being wrong in an options trade: If the underlying price doesn't move into a position where you can make money by exercising the option, you lose just the option premium. This reduces the risk of loss considerably. However, you will lose the option premium amount no matter what.

Therefore, your exit on successful trades needs to overcome this amount.

6. The closer the underlying price is to the strike price, the more expensive the option will be. Try to buy options that are some distance away from the underlying. This way, you'll earn more.

7. Remember that a single contract covers 100 underlying shares. Multiply the price of the option by 100 to arrive at its true purchase cost.

8. You will need to open a margin account to trade options. I'll detail this in the next chapter.

Futures

Futures contracts are the other type of derivative you will be trading in the market. A futures contract is different from an option, even though a single contract covers 100 underlying shares. Like options, futures have a monthly expiry date. However, they don't have premiums attached to them. Instead, their prices mimic movements in the underlying price and are usually close to it. A futures contract is a promise, from the seller to the buyer, that they will deliver the underlying to the buyer at the price the buyer paid when purchasing.

For example: If you buy WMT futures at $60 that expire on June 30th, the seller of the contract is agreeing to sell you WMT at $60 on June 30th, should you choose to exercise the contract. While you can let options expire worthless after the expiry date, this is not the case with futures.

Trading them is a lot like trading the underlying stock. You will need to manually exit the trade for a profit or loss. The contract's price before the expiry date will be close to, but different, from the underlying price. However, on the expiry date, both prices will converge towards one another.

So, what's the advantage of trading futures over the underlying stock? For one thing futures allow you to leverage your purchase. Every stock has its own leverage rates and these are fixed by the broker. Whatever the leverage rate is, the fact remains that you can put down a fraction of the money required to trade 100 shares of the underlying, and boost your returns.

Futures are typically settled on a cash basis. This means your account will be credited and debited every day depending on whether the instrument rose or fell in value. You will need to keep a sharp eye on your margin levels, which I'll discuss in the next chapter.

There is another concept that occurs in the world of futures to understand, called a rollover. Futures exist for multiple months. For example, WMT will have futures contracts expiring in June, July and August. All these contracts will have different prices. If you trade the June contract and think that you want to hold on to it for longer than a month, you can do this using a rollover. On the expiry date of the June contract, you simply rollover your position to the July contract and your position is kept alive. Rollovers are not typically practiced in options, but they're used quite a lot in futures.

While I mentioned you should not be shorting options, you can do so with futures. They're just like common stock except they contain leverage within them. You'll need to make sure your risk management is up to scratch and that you're not risking an amount that will bankrupt you.

This brings to a close our look at derivatives within the stock market. There are many more derivatives that exist in the financial markets. In fact, options alone have more than just two types. Sticking to these choices is recommended because, with derivatives, things can get complicated in a hurry.

Simplicity is the key to trading them well. Stick to calls and puts and always keep an eye on your margin as instructed in the next chapter. Derivatives have been called weapons of mass destruction by long-term buy and hold investors, and this is true to a certain extent.

Instead of calling them WMDs, a better analogy is to think of them as being extremely powerful racing cars. These cars can achieve levels of performance that are impossible for road going cars and are finely tuned pieces of engineering. However, if the driver isn't qualified enough to take them out for a spin, they'll likely end up in the wall in a heap of metal.

Similarly, you need to practice your skills before taking derivatives out for a spin. Don't underestimate the danger they pose to your trading account. I highlighted previously how leverage can boost gains but it boosts losses as well. In my previous example, I mentioned how a 1% gain in the underlying price leads to a 100% gain for your account. However, a 1% decline in underlying price will lead to a 100% loss for your account as well. All derivatives contain an element of leverage and this makes them extremely dangerous to trade if you don't know what you're doing.

This is not to say trading them well is impossible. It's just that you need to practice your skills according to the seven steps I'll show you later in this book.

For now, let's move on and take a look at why you should be swing trading.

Types of Trading

There are many different ways to make money in the markets. I've already highlighted how buy and hold works. As the name suggests, you buy a stock and hold on forever. Within trading there are different ways of making money as well. These can be classified as:

1. Day trading
2. Swing trading
3. Options trading

4.   Scalping

Day trading involves holding on to your position for a single market session. In the case of forex, you could hold on through multiple sessions as well. The key point day traders focus on is called gap risk.

A gap forms when the price at which the stock opens in the next session is different from the price at which it ended the previous one. Most novices to the markets assume that prices move in a single chain of interconnected prices. This isn't the case. Prices can and do jump all over the place without touching anything in between.

For example, WMT can close at $100 today and open at $110 tomorrow. This $10 difference is the gap. On the charts, thanks to the way price is depicted, you will see a gap and this is where the name comes from. The FX markets are open 24 hours a day and gaps don't occur overnight.

However, they do occur during the day, thanks to special events such as interest rate announcements, fiscal policy announcements, payroll reports and other political events. Day traders in FX have to take these into account when building their strategies. Usually, the day trader simply stays away from such announcements by closing their position before it happens.

While day traders insulate themselves from gap risk, they also reduce the amount of money they can make over time. After all, there's only so far a stock can move over a single session. While it's true that stocks can fall less over a day than over a year, this is negated by the fact that day traders usually pay large commissions to their brokers, due to the number of trades they execute.

In order to make a large number of gains, day traders necessarily have to place many trades. This drives costs upwards and results in additional barriers to overcome. Good day traders tend to be among the very best traders in their profession. However, the learning curve is steep and it calls for a lot of dedication and effort to achieve this.

For this reason, many beginner traders adopt swing trading tactics. Swing trading is when a trader holds on to a position for up to a week and for more than a day. Some define swing trading as holding on to positions for a month, but this is incorrect. The swing trader aims to capture the price swing that occurs over the course of a single day or a few days.

Swing trading is less hectic than day trading because of the large time frames involved. In day trading, the trader is focused on watching price movements every five to fifteen minutes. With swing trading, the trader can check in every hour or even four hours. This allows them to do something else with their time while the markets move.

Another huge advantage to swing trading is that it provides a good amount of feedback to the beginner trader while keeping the pace of decision-making low. Beginners need constant feedback in order to learn their art, and swing trading delivers this at a palatable rate without overwhelming them like day trading does.

The next type of trading is options trading. These strategies are completely different from day and swing trading strategies. Note that you can swing and day trade options premiums as I'll show you in this book. However, the majority of options strategies take advantage of volatility.

Volatility refers to how much fluctuation there is in prices in the market. A market that rises quickly is said to be volatile. One that jumps up and down violently is also volatile. Options allow the trader to bet on the volatility itself instead of the price. Thus, the trader is non-directional in terms of price movement.

They don't care about whether prices go up or down, they're only concerned with the degree of movement and whether this will reduce or increase. As you can see, this is complicated stuff. Trading options via such volatility strategies is not for the weak. They utilize the full power of options and you need to have expertise in trading to understand them completely.

Beginners are best off avoiding them as a result. However, you should expand into them once you've made money with swing trading since options volatility strategies are a brilliant way to boost your returns.

Lastly, we have scalping and this is perhaps the least profitable way for the retail trader to trade. Scalping involves jumping in and out of positions quickly, often for mere seconds. These days, given the speed with which markets move, all scalpers use algorithms.

This tactic should sound familiar to you. It is exactly what HFT firms do. When the retail trader takes their fancy algorithm out for a spin in the market, they're pitting themselves against billion dollar companies that are doing the same thing. Who do you think is going to win? A billion dollar company or the retail trader with $5,000 worth of capital in their account? The answer is obvious.

Swing Trading Versus Investing

Due to the lengthier holding times, a few traders end up confusing swing trading with buy and hold investing. Let's get a few facts clear: Trading, be it swing or day trading is nothing like buy and hold investing. The approaches are totally different. For starters, buy and hold investors look to hang onto their investments for decades.

There isn't a single trader on the planet who seeks to hold their position for more than a few weeks at the most. Options traders who look to take advantage of volatility hang onto their trades for a month at the most. The timelines involved are nowhere close, as you can see.

Next is the approach that is adopted to downswings in price. When a buy and hold investor witnesses the price of their investment dipping below their purchase level, their approach is to hang onto their investment and possibly even buy more. This is because they base their buying decisions on long term fundamental factors.

These factors are tied to the quality of the company's business and the sector outlook for the company. It has nothing to do with the emotions that drive prices. Trading is a means of trying to profit from the emotional swings that result in stock price movements. This calls for the exact opposite approach.

Since the trader isn't keen on holding on for a long time, they're looking to exist at preset points. This means their stop loss levels and take profit levels are set in stone. If the price of the instrument exceeds their stop loss, they exit without a moment's hesitation. There is no thought of allowing the price to bounce back up or anything of the sort.

Take profit levels are maximized and are determined on the basis of the risk involved in the trade. They aren't connected to fundamental business factors. While buy and hold investors concern themselves with the quality of management and other factors surrounding the business, the average trade isn't concerned with this. You don't even need to know the company's name to profit from it!

Some people get misled by movie depictions of traders who are geniuses and know everything about the company. They know that a new drug is coming to the market and that the CEO is having an affair with the

CFO and this is going to boost stock prices. In real life, traders don't worry about any such news items.

They know that, in the short term, prices adjust to reflect current news cycles. The markets are efficient over the short term, and it's unlikely that you're going to find huge opportunities by reading a newspaper. In fact, by doing this you'll lose money. By the time the news is printed in the paper, it's too late to make any significant difference.

Should you then try to get inside news on a company through nefarious means? You're welcome to try! You'll risk being jailed is all. Instead, it's far better to stay away from the news except in certain special situations as I'll show you later in this book. You can also take advantage of certain instruments that have traditionally been the stronghold of buy and hold investing.

Keep these points in mind as you read the rest of this book. You are not an investor in the traditional sense of the word. You're an intelligent speculator. Your concern is with the short-term movements of financial instruments and swing trading is how you take advantage of these movements.

It's important to keep this in mind because many traders become inadvertent investors when they start believing that their losing positions will return to profit or that they need to remove their stop losses and so on. All of this is just a way to lose money. It is also how many traders speculate unintelligently.

Now that you've understood the basics about the market, it's time to understand how brokers and the regulations surrounding the markets work.

Chapter 2:

Rules and Regulations

While trading is an open space that allows you to operate any strategy you can think of, there are certain rules that you need to abide by. The one that is the most well-known is the insider information rule. You cannot trade on the basis of insider information and the penalties for doing this are harsh.

As a retail trader, it's unlikely you'll be in a position to take advantage of such information anyway. The markets are regulated by overlapping bodies and the lines between them get blurred. However, between them they manage to keep the markets in check, and as a retail trader you can rest assured that your money is safe.

The primary organization that governs the markets is the Securities and Exchange Commission (SEC). The SEC cops the brunt of criticism when a financial crisis occurs since they have oversight on all trading activities in the market. Closely allied with the SEC is the Financial Industry Regulatory Authority (FINRA). FINRA regulates the institutions participating in the markets.

Brokers, for example, are subject to FINRA regulations, as are people who manage other people's money. This authority conducts a variety of licensing exams that professionals have to take. The license also comes with a code of conduct that needs to be adhered to. Any violation of this results in fines and consequences of Biblical proportions.

The FX space is regulated by the Commodities and Futures Trading Commissions (CFTC) and the National Futures Association (NFA). As you can tell by the word futures in their names, they have purview over derivatives as well. Options and futures trading activities fall under their jurisdiction.

The CFTC is responsible for monitoring brokerage activity in FX. FX brokerage is a bit different from stock brokering, as you'll learn shortly. The NFA is an organization that monitors all professional activities in the market, aside from just brokers, and prescribes a strict code of conduct.

Between these four bodies, the American markets are heavily regulated. I'm taking the time to explain the role of these bodies because far too many retail traders are under the impression that the markets are corrupt, and that there's no way retail traders can make money.

This usually happens after a string of losses and the emotional upheaval they cause. Instead of blaming your broker or the market, examine your own trading practices. That's where the fault lies.

A regulation that you must be aware of is the PDT rule or Pattern Day Trading rule. This has significant implications for your trading capital. This rule is defined by FINRA and is enforced by the SEC. Here's what the SEc's website tells us about this designation ("Pattern Day Trader", 2020):

FINRA rules define a "pattern day trader" as any customer who executes four or more "day trades" within five business days, provided that the number of day trades represents more than six percent of the customer's total trades in the margin account for that same five business day period.

The rules further state that if a broker has a reasonable belief that a customer will engage in day trading, they can designate them with the PDT tag. How does this impact you?

The biggest impact is that you will need to maintain a minimum balance of $25,000 in your account if you're going to be hit with this. This is a large amount of capital, and most readers will likely not have this amount of money to trade with. Is there any way of getting around this?

There are two ways you can do this. The first is to recognize that this is an SEC and FINRA rule, which means that the FX markets are not covered by them. Restricting yourself to trading FX solely, is a good way forward. At first, it is the most practical way to trade and to build your capital up to a level where you won't need to worry about PDT.

The second and less practical way, is to trade just one instrument in the stock market. It could be an option, a futures contract or common stock of a single company, and to enter into a position no more than twice a week. There are many pitfalls of this method and I don't recommend you do it.

For starters, you won't know how often opportunity will knock. It might come on all five days or it might come just once a month. By restricting yourself, you're moving out of sync with the market. Next, the fact that you're restricting yourself to just one stock means you'll miss other opportunities.

To truly trade the market well, you need to be able to trade without any restrictions or worries on trade limits. Instead of trying to work around PDT in the stock market, move to FX instead. You'll be able to trade using sound principles and will be able to grow your money faster.

Now that we've looked at regulations, let's turn our attention towards brokers.

Brokers

Stock brokers differ from FX brokers in many ways. You'll learn about these differences shortly. Before we get there, it's important for you to recognize who your broker is. Brokers get a fair amount of stick from traders and this usually happens because they don't understand the true function of a broker.

Here's a simple method to check whether you understand what a broker's function is: If you happen to be in a bind and not have any trade ideas, do you think asking your broker for some is a worthwhile option? If you answer yes to this question, then you've got some learning to do!

Your broker's sole duty is to execute your trades. That's it. This applies whether they're a stock market broker or an FX broker. They aren't there to give you advice or to guide you with regard to the ins and outs of the stock market. This is where many traders make a mistake.

They believe that just because the broker is providing them with access to the market, they must be experts in it as well. Your broker doesn't know anything more than the average person in the street when it comes to trading. Their job is to execute your trades and to keep you happy. Whether you lose or make money is beside the point.

In this era of commission free trades, the broker's job is to direct you towards other products in their organization. If you fail to make money with trading you might find your broker directing you towards their IRA products and other financial schemes they might be running.

There are brokers out there that cater solely to traders. You'll find that these brokers are very different from the Schwab and TD Ameritrade's of the world. They stick to the belief that the trader is a business person, and that the brokerage operations are a different business.

The fact is that brokerage commissions are a cost for your trading business. In fact, after taxes, these are your biggest costs. Your broker works for you and isn't your friend or confidant. So stop thinking that you can rely on them for advice. They're a salesperson at best and should be treated as a cost.

Slippage

A common scenario that causes many retail traders to lose patience with their brokers is slippage. Slippage is when you place an order to buy stock at $100, and see that your order was filled for $105. The average losing retail trader immediately yells conspiracy and floods trading forums online about how the broker is dishonest.

Slippage is a constant risk in the market and there's no avoiding this. It occurs during times of high volatility. In such times, the market reevaluates which price levels are justified, and as a result, liquidity evaporates. Liquidity refers to how easily an instrument can be traded.

Gaps are also an example of slippage in action. You may have placed your stop loss order at $100, but if there was no market at that price, there's nothing your broker can do. The prices you see on screen are not real. They're an accurate representation of what just happened.

There's no way for you to accurately pinpoint where the market is currently priced. Sure, you can estimate this with decent levels of accuracy most of the time. However, don't mistake the flurry of numbers on your trading software for accuracy. During volatile times, prices vanish and you will experience slippage.

One easy way of avoiding slippage is to stay away from moments of high volatility. If you know an event is coming up that will create volatility, you can steer clear of this. Another way is to use the orders your broker provides you with. Many traders don't pay enough attention to this facet of trading so let's examine this now.

Order Types

These orders are available irrespective of whether you're trading with an FX or stock market broker. The most common type of order available is the market order. When you place this order, you're instructing your broker to capture whatever price you find in the market.

For example, if you place an order of 100 shares of WMT at market, your broker will buy 100 shares no matter what the market price is. If the price when buying the first 50 shares is $50, the next 30 shares is $60 and the last 20 shares is $40, then these are the prices at which your order will be executed.

In short, you're not insulated from volatility. Market orders are useful in that they get you into your position quickly and you're guaranteed a fill irrespective of price. If you want to exit your position, they're equally useful.

The problem with market orders is that they're instantaneous, and require you to be present at all times to execute them. To address this problem, limit orders were developed. A limit order can be set ahead of time because it contains a trigger. Once the market breaches this trigger, your broker will execute your order for as long as the market remains on the favorable side of the trigger.

For example, if you wanted to buy 100 shares of WMT but wanted to pay no more than $50 for them, your broker will buy as much WMT as available when the price dips below $50. If you were shorting 100 WMT, they would sell all the WMT above $50. The limit order ensures you receive the best price possible depending on the direction of your trade.

There is a catch with limit orders. While you're guaranteed the best price possible, you're not guaranteed a complete fill. If your broker finds just 30 shares below $50 for WMT then this will be the size of your position unless you manually intervene and buy the rest at market.

This makes limit orders wholly unsuited for stop loss orders. When the trade has moved against you and you want to get out at all costs, limit orders will not guarantee a full exit. To address this problem stop orders were created.

Stop orders also contain a trigger price. The difference between them and limit orders is that once the trigger is breached by the market, the entire quantity specified in the order is bought or sold no matter the price.

Let's say you have a sell stop order on WMT at $50 for 100 shares. In this case, you're telling your broker that the minute WMT dips below $50, they need to sell 100 shares and get you out of the market no matter what. If WMT jumps up to $55 after hitting 50, then you'll still sell all 100 shares at the prices available.

As you can see, none of these orders are perfect. However, by using a combination of them when trading, you can reduce your risk significantly. The type of order you will use depends on the kind of strategy you're utilizing. At the very least, you can infer this much: When setting a maximum loss level for your trade, using a stop order is the best.

This ensures you'll get out of the position and won't turn into an accidental investor. A stop loss order is an example of a stop order. Keep in mind that when you go short, your stop loss order will be a buy stop order. If you're long, your stop loss will be a sell stop order.

There are many more order types that brokers provide, especially the ones that cater to traders. There isn't an official count but a conservative estimate would place these order types to be over 100. An example of an advanced order type is the iceberg order. This is where you declare a nominal position size you're looking to buy, but instruct the broker that the real size is more than that.

Hence, the true size of your order is hidden. Traders used to employ this order to take advantage of HFT algorithms. However, given that these firms are the exchanges' biggest clients, it should come as no surprise that these days using iceberg orders to manipulate order flow is illegal.

My point is that order types are extremely powerful and will have an impact on your bottom line, so you need to build your skill levels up to a point where you're qualified to use them properly. Before you reach this level, use market, limit and stop orders to help manage your entry and exit risk.

Account Types

With stock market brokers you can open a cash account or a margin account. Margin accounts are needed to short stocks. The account minimums for these accounts are higher. Some discount brokers offer accounts with minimums of $5,000, while some expect you to deposit the PDT minimum of $25,000.

You might be tempted to trade using just a cash account, but this is a lot like trying to trade your way around PDT. Don't do this. Instead, focus on trading FX. Of course, that opens you up to the far more entertaining world of FX brokerage.

The Deal With FX Brokers

FX brokerage in the US used to be a Wild West experience. There were no steady laws, and leverage up to 1:500 used to be available. Thankfully, all of that nonsense was shutdown earlier this decade, and the space is now relatively sedate. While the international FX brokerage is still highly suspect, in the U.S. you can rest assured that brokers are above board and highly regulated.

For starters, you will receive 1:50 leverage and not more than this. This is to protect you, as well as the broker. After all, they're risking their own capital when it comes to FX. A holdover from the dark days of FX trading is the concept of B booking. This has been cloaked with the more marketing friendly term 'Hybrid models.'

Here's how it works: An FX broker knows the statistics when it comes to how likely you are to go bust in under a year. The broker does not make a lot of money executing your trades. A standard lot round trip (buying and selling) generates around 16 cents in commissions.

They have two options to make money from you. The first is to get you to trade more. Every broker, even stock market ones, do this by sending you newsletters and pinging you with news feeds in your trading terminal. This encourages emotional trading and you generate commissions for them.

The second, more profitable option is to B book your trades. This is when the broker assumes the other side of your trades instead of executing them. I mentioned earlier that a broker's fiduciary duty is to execute your trades, not trade against you. The SEC and FINRA take a dim view of this when it comes to the stock markets.

However, since FX doesn't come under their purview, a few brokers practice this, and it puts them in a serious conflict of interest with their clients. The reason behind the broker opting for B booking is very simple. Statistically, a new trader is more likely to fail than succeed, especially if their account size is less than $10,000.

This means they're going to be wrong in their trade judgment, more often than not. The person on the other side of their trades is going to be successful, more often than not. Therefore, instead of passing your trade onto the open market, the broker takes the other side of the trade and buys or sells the instrument to you.

For example, if you want to buy 1.1 EURUSD, and if the broker B books you, they'll buy 1.1 EURUSD from the open market at 1.2345 and sell it to you for 1.2347. Your long position is now initiated at 1.2347. Notice that the broker has already made a two pip profit on this trade by selling EURUSD at an inflated price.

If you happen to be wrong and exit your trade by selling 1.1 EURUSD, they'll buy it back from you and sell it back onto the open market. Thus, a neat profit is made. Now imagine replicating this over thousands of traders, and you can see why B booking is profitable.

It also happens to be illegal in the stock market. Like I said, FX is a different world and it's permitted for now. Here are some tell-tale signs of a B booker:

1. They offer commission free trades. While you want to see this in the stock market, you need to run away from it when it comes to FX. Commission free simply means your broker will sell instruments to you at an inflated price.

2. They talk about hybrid order execution models. Hybrid equals B booking. In this case, hybrid means they route a few orders into the open market to their LPs (A book) while they B book the rest. If they have 100 orders and A book

one, while B booking 99, technically they're a hybrid broker.

Look for ECN or STP brokers. ECN stands for Electronic Communication Network while STP stands for Straight Through Processing. These types of brokers send your orders directly to their LP, and don't have dealing desks trading against you.

While this isn't a big deal in America, make sure your FX broker provides you with New York close charts. These charts treat 5 P.M. EST as being the end of the forex day. You want to do this because this is traditionally when forex volumes drop off, and it is a logical end to the forex day.

It also standardizes the sessions and price action well. If you had London close charts, then your chart would look different. This will lead you to spotting patterns incorrectly. Think of it as searching for something on Google and receiving a censored version of results instead of the real results.

If you're based in America, then all brokers will default to New York close charts. It still pays to ask them about it.

International forex brokers will also offer you an instrument called a CFD. CFD stands for contracts for difference. These are not allowed in the United States. CFDs are B booking havens since they are broker-generated contracts that mimic the moves of another instrument, such as a financial index or futures contract.

They aren't complicated to trade, but given the high levels of leverage they involve, plus the B booking aspect, it's best to stay away from them as much as possible.

Price Spreads

I mentioned previously that the prices you see on a chart aren't real. Constant market action means that the prices you see on screen are constantly changing, and it's impossible to keep up with every minute change.

There's another reason for those prices not being real. Prices in the market aren't a single number. Every instrument is priced in a band that is called the spread. The spread has two prices within it. One is a buying price called the Ask, and the other is the selling price called the Bid.

You'll usually see something like WMT 50.5/50.75 as a price quote for a stock. This quote indicates that you can buy WMT at $50.75, and sell it for $50.50 per share. The spread, in this case, is 25 cents.

During times of high volatility or low liquidity, the spread will widen. Wide spreads are something to stay away from because it will hamper your ability to exit profitably. For example, if WMT's spread was 50.5/100, WMT's bid will have to reach $100 before you can even think about selling. If it rises all the way up to $70, you cannot sell profitably because you bought it for $100.

While the above example is extreme, especially for a stock like WMT, situations like these happen all the time in FX. This is why you need to stick to the major pairs, or trade the minor ones when their home markets are online. Trade outside of the regular times and you'll get hit with a wide spread and a useless position.

Chapter 3:

Candles and Prices

It's now time for you to learn all about the world of candlestick charting. Candlesticks are the most powerful way to read price charts, and most traders tend to use them. If you've never used candlesticks before, then you're about to enter a whole new world where you'll gain huge insight into the way price really moves in the market.

The most common form of price depiction used in the markets is a line. If you switch on CNBC you'll usually see an important looking chart where price is shown as being a graph with a line of it. This line can have crests and dips and looks intelligent enough. However, a line chart communicates almost nothing of value to you as a trader. Much like the financial media.

Prices are not stationary and fluctuate all the time. The typical line chart gives you a snapshot of the closing prices of an instrument. There are four parts to an instrument's price: Open, high, low and close. Together all of these are called the OHLC. Traders need to take all four components of price into account, in order to make good decisions.

All price charts provide a snapshot of price action that is relevant to a certain timeframe. For example, a daily chart (D1) will show you what happens on a daily basis. A weekly chart (W1) will consolidate the D1 price action into weekly buckets and will display the price action accordingly.

Below the D1, you'll encounter either the four-hour chart (H4) or the 60-minute chart (H1). In the case of FX, you will have to pay attention to the H4. With stocks, the H4 is usually not displayed and the H1 is paid attention to. Below the H1, you have the 30-minute chart (M30), 15 minute (M15), 5 minute (M5) and 1 Minute (M1).

Swing traders typically stick to the H1, H4 and D1 timeframes. This applies whether you're trading FX or stocks. If you're trading the H1, you'll need to check back with the market every hour to figure out what to do next and whether the market changed in any way.

A line chart is constructed in the following manner. Let's use the H1 as an example. If the market opens at 9 A.M., then the first compartment of price action on this chart is the block between 9 A.M. and 10 A.M. Whatever the price is at 10 A.M., that's the closing price or the close of that block. A solitary dot is plotted on a graph of time versus price.

Next the closing price of the 10 A.M. to 11 A.M. block is plotted. The two dots are joined to one another and, in this manner, a line chart is created. Financial news channels usually show you a tick chart as well. The tick chart is pretty much useless to you as a trader. It plots literally every single tick or price fluctuation in the market, as and when it occurs. Given the speed with which transactions occur these days, tick charts are on an even lower timeframe than the M1.

Going back to our example, within the 9-10 A.M. block, price isn't stationary. It keeps jumping around. For example, at 9 A.M. the price could be 100. At 9:30 A.M. it could be 150. At 10 A.M. it could be 90. The line chart captures all of these moves as a solitary dot at 90.

This is why OHLC is so important, and candlesticks are the best way of capturing all of this information. Let's take a look at how they do this.

Candlestick Structure

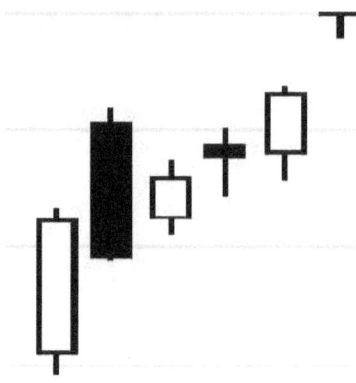

Figure 1 - Candlesticks

Figure 1 illustrates five candlesticks. These have been taken from the daily chart of AAPL. There are two types of candlesticks here. One type is colored white and the other black. White candles are bullish and black ones are bearish. You can set this up any way you like in your charting software. In all examples in this book, this is how I've set it up.

Let's look at the white candles first. We'll begin by looking at the body of the candle, the rectangular shape that is colored white. The bottom of the body is the open, and the top is the close. You'll notice that there are vertical lines sticking out from the top and bottom of the body.

The vertical line on top is called the wick, and the one on the bottom is called the tail. The highest extent of the wick is the high, while the lowest extent of the tail is the low. By looking at the candle, you can immediately tell where the OHLC points are.

In the case of the bearish candles, the wicks and tails represent that same thing. However, the order of the open and close is flipped. In this case, the open is the upper boundary of the body, and the close is at the bottom of the body. Price begins this particular session (which is a day since this is a D1 chart and every candle represents one day's worth of price action) on top and then falls to a lower level. Thus, the close is lower than the high.

Bearish bars will have their close below their open, while bullish bars will have their close above their open (since price increases in their case.)

Another feature to notice in Figure 1 is that the size of the candle bodies vary. The first two candles, which are bullish and bearish respectively, are sized the same. However, the ones that follow are smaller in size. This is despite every candle representing a single day's worth of price action. It just goes to show how much variance there can be in price action between days.

In order to compare the information provided by the candlestick chart to a line chart, go ahead and draw a line through all the closing prices in Figure 1. Compare the two charts, and you'll notice how much more information is provided by the candlestick chart.

The size of the bar is important to note because it conveys important order flow information. In fact, the structure of the candle itself conveys a lot of information about how buyers and sellers are placed in the market. Let's take the first two bars from the left as an example.

The first candle is bullish and has a strong body. I say strong because it doesn't have much of a wick. The bullish traders pushed prices up enough so that the close ended up being near the high. The fact that there's no tail indicates that the bears didn't push prices low or simply didn't have the chance to do so.

The second candle is bearish. For starters notice how much higher its open is than the previous close. What must have happened is that the bulls must have built up pressure overnight, and prices must have gapped on the open. However, this much demand was clearly unjustified. Prices came tumbling down, and eventually the bears managed to push prices below the previous day's close.

Notice the small wick on top of the bearish candle. This indicates the bulls tried pushing prices higher but were harshly rejected by the bears. Also notice how the close of this candle is equal to the low. It shows that the bulls barely got a word in throughout the day.

All market prices are the result of bulls and bears constantly pushing against one another. As traders, our job is to figure out who has the upper hand, and to join that side of the market. It isn't to pick a side and then become a cheerleader for it. This is what a lot of novice traders do.

They enter a position and then begin cheering every single tick in their favor. Keeping an open mind will help you spot if you're wrong in your analysis. For example, if you find that your long position is in error, you can swiftly exit the position and go short instead and make money.

Getting back to Figure 1, the next three bars are much smaller in size. The small size indicates less price fluctuation, and given that all three of them have an upward tilt, it probably means that the bulls are pushing steadily against the bears. Towards the right-hand edge of the chart, you can see a gap form as AAPL explodes higher. The final candle is not fully shown but you see its bottom extremity on the top right.

By depicting OHLC in this manner, you manage to extract a lot of information from the market. Keep in mind that this is just five bars/candles (terms are used interchangeably) we've looked at so far. Imagine what an entire chart worth of price bars will do for you!

I must mention that your objective isn't to dissect every single bar on the chart. Doing so would result in an overload of information, and you'll likely confuse yourself. Instead, you need to figure out what's going on by looking at candles within a larger framework. This is the range/trend framework that I'll discuss in the next chapter.

While the framework turbocharges your ability to analyze the market, you can use candlesticks all by themselves. There are certain order flow patterns that candlesticks depict. By spotting these you can make reasonable assumptions about the direction in which the market will move next.

Inside Bars

The first pattern we'll look at are inside bars. Candlestick patterns are quite numerous. Given that they're of Japanese origin a lot of them have funny names such as a hanging man and shooting star and so on. Many traders memorize these patterns and then try to apply them on a chart, as if trading was a matter of geometry.

Resist the urge to do this. Instead, dig deeper and figure out what the order flow situation is behind the pattern. When you're trading a chart, your first objective is to figure out whether prices are going to continue in a certain direction or whether they're going to reverse.

Inside bars are a continuation pattern. Sometimes they can indicate reversal as well. To spot these reversals you need to understand the trend/range framework, so I'll stay away from these for now. Continuation patterns by themselves are extremely powerful, so it isn't as if you're going to miss any opportunities.

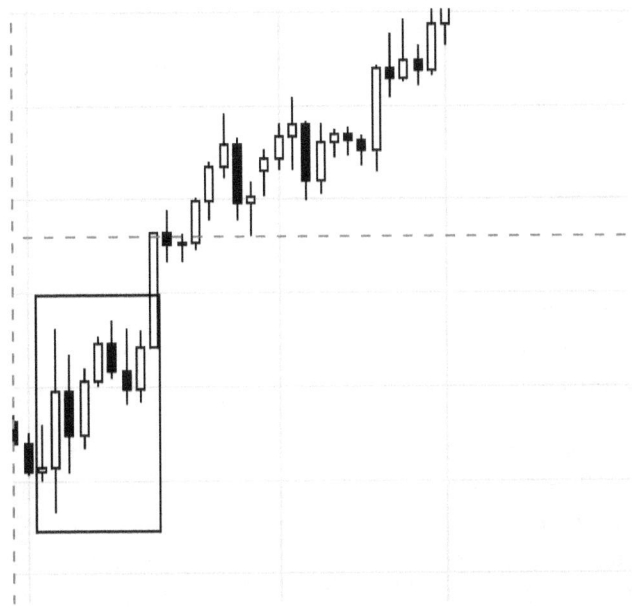

Figure 2: Inside Bar Cluster

Figure 2 illustrates an inside bar cluster within the rectangle. We have a bullish bar with a significant tail and a wick. The six bars that follow it are all inside bars. They're designated as such because all of them fall within the confines of the first large bar.

Technically speaking, the fourth bar's wick peeks out above the large bar's high, but given how small this violation is, it doesn't mean much in terms of order flow.

The inside bar pattern is a two bar pattern at the very least. The first bar in the pattern is large and can be bullish or bearish. The direction of this first bar determines which direction price will continue in. In addition to this, you want to pay attention to the overall direction in which price is moving prior to the first large bar.

The direction of the second and subsequent inside bars, isn't too important. What is important is that those bars are smaller in extent than the large bar, and that they exist within its confines. The more bars that exist inside the extent of the larger bar, the more powerful the pattern is.

What does an inside bar communicate to us from an order flow perspective? The large bar in a given direction, tells us that the traders backing that side of the market are strong. In the case of Figure 2, it is the bulls that are strong. The presence of the large tail and wick reduces this view of strength quite a lot.

However, the subsequent inside bars confirm this strength. The smaller bars convey that bulls and bears are locked in a tight struggle within a small space. If the bulls were weak, then the bears would have no problems pushing prices back down below the original bullish bar. This is clearly not the case here.

While the first inside bar is bearish, the subsequent ones result in prices being pushed higher. As a result, we can surmise that whatever the strength of the bulls might be, the bears are clearly weak. This means prices have only one way to go, and that's up.

You can see how prices break out and move higher following the inside bar cluster. Notice how forcefully the bulls push above the upper boundary of the cluster. This indicates how strong they were, and how weak the bears were.

Inside bars are best used in trends. You should never use these in ranges since their potency is dulled under such conditions. You'll learn what trends and ranges are in the next chapter so keep this in mind when moving forward.

Pin Bars

Pin bars are perhaps the easiest price pattern to spot on a chart. The structure of a pin bar is quite simple. It is a bar with a small body and has either a long tail or a long wick. Pin bars with long wicks are bearish in nature, and pins with long tails are bullish in nature.

Despite them being easy to spot, they aren't straightforward to trade. This has led to pin bars acquiring a notorious reputation of being false indicators. The problem is that most traders don't understand how they're supposed to use them and end up using them at inappropriate times. First, let's look at an example of a pin bar.

Figure 3 - Pin Bars at A and B

Figure 3 illustrates two sets of pin bars. At A, we have a bullish pin bar and at B we have two bearish pin bars. Notice that the direction of the candle body itself doesn't matter when determining bullishness or bearishness. At A, you can see how much larger the tail is compared to the body.

The same is the case at B. What is different between A and B is the way in which you'll trade them. Pin bars are meant to be traded as continuations. This advice is contrary to what you'll receive from most trading books. You'll be told that they're great reversal patterns.

Trading pin bars as reversals is only going to result in you amassing gargantuan losses. It isn't easy to predict reversals ahead of time so stay away from trying to do this. Instead, use them as continuation patterns.

To understand how to do this, look for trends to begin with. Any market that is headed in a particular direction is trending. In Figure 3,you can see that the trend is up before price even reaches A. It takes a momentary sideways breather here, and this is your best chance to get in on the powerful uptrend.

Notice how the pin is formed after a strong bearish bar. This isn't a coincidence. From a price action perspective, the bulls have been in control for a long time, and the bears step in while the bulls take a breather. They manage to print a strong bearish bar but the bulls step right back in.

The large tail on the pin bar tells us that bears tried pushing prices lower but were repulsed by the bulls. Ultimately, the bulls pushed prices all the way back above the open. This is a pretty strong indication that they're still in charge. Subsequent price action reveals that this was the right judgment call.

In a sense, A is a reversal signal. It just doesn't indicate the kind of reversal most traders are looking for. It indicates a reversal of the short term, bearish pressure in the larger bull trend. Thus, the pin at A is a continuation pattern.

Now let's take a look at the two pins at B. Unfortunately, most traders blindly trade every pin bar that appears on the chart. The pins at B are the ones that undo most profits that traders manage to accumulate. For starters, these are bearish pins due to the fact that they have wicks.

The color of their bodies is not important. When you look at these two in isolation, the price action indicates that bulls tried pushing prices higher, but the bears stepped in and pushed them right back down. So far, so good.

The problem in trading these pins and using them as short indicators is that it makes no sense when you view the entire picture. There is a strong uptrend in place. This uptrend has lasted for a large number of bars. Look at the size of the push upwards from the bottom of Figure 3. I must mention that Figure 3 is a continuation of Figure 2 so this uptrend begins all the way from there.

Do you really think that two small pin bars can overturn such a large trend? What is the footprint of this huge uptrend versus those two pins at B? Notice how the bulls barely glance at the pins at B and keep moving prices past them anyway.

Using pins as reversal indicators is a silly thing to do if you don't consider the overall trend. It places far too much importance on the geometric shape of the indicator instead of figuring out what the overall picture is.

Use them to spot the times when you can enter with the trend safely, and you'll find that you'll make money a lot more easily.

Engulfing Bars

These are also called outside bars. This is a two bar pattern. The first bar is the smaller one and is engulfed by the one to its right. The direction of the second, outside bar is what determines the direction of the signal. If it happens to be bullish, then it's a bullish signal.

Unlike the previous two patterns, engulfing bars are reversal indicators. What's more they're extremely reliable and tend to form when trends end. Don't expect price to go rocketing away in the opposite direction, though. What usually happens is that engulfing bars form right at the end of the trending movement.

Price then moves into a range, as you'll learn in the next chapter. The engulfing bar allows you to enter right when the trend ends, and you can pocket a quick profit as price bounces the other way and begins to move sideways. As a result, your holding times for this pattern are a lot shorter than with the other ones.

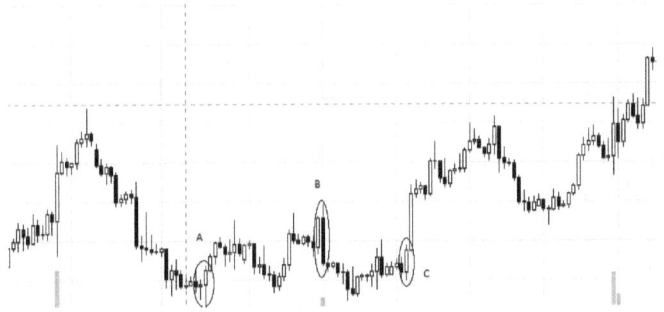

Figure 4 - Three Engulfing Bars

Figure 4 illustrates what both bullish and bearish engulfing bars look like. These are marked by the letters A, B and C, and much like pin bars, it is possible to trade engulfing bars incorrectly.

First, we have the engulfing bar at A. The body of the larger bar is small but it has a significant tail. As such, you could make a case for this being a valid pin bar as well. Advanced traders would probably mark this as such. However, since you won't be trading pins as reversal signals, it's best to consider this as an engulfing pattern.

Notice how it engulfs, not just the first bar on its left, but multiple bars to its left. This indicates that the bearish pressure is receding and that the bulls are literally overshadowing the bears. The presence of the tail further adds strength to our case.

It's important for you to look for engulfing bars only in ranges that form at the end of trends. You might spot them within trends, but these aren't as powerful and offer you less than efficient entries. You'll learn all about trends and ranges in the next chapter, so just remember this point for now.

The second engulfing bar we see in figure 4 is the one at B. Here, we have a bearish pattern since the larger bar is bearish. While this is a picture perfect engulfing pattern visually, does this mean it's a valid signal? Consider first that the engulfing pattern is a reversal.

We're in a situation where a bearish trend has ended or is ending, and we've already seen a bullish engulfing pattern produce an upswing. Clearly the bulls are steadily overpowering the bears. Does it make sense to go short in such times, on this chart? Clearly not! After all, the bears are steadily losing ground. If they were still strong, there wouldn't be a range in the first place. We'd still witness prices moving downwards instead of sideways.

This makes the signal at B an invalid one. Then we have the signal at C. In terms of size, this is the smaller, but notice how it occurs on pretty much the same level as the signal at A. This is a pretty strong sign that the bulls are defending this level strongly. Whenever the bears push into it, they get engulfed by the bulls.

Figure 4 also shows how you often need patience with engulfing patterns. Notice how long an entry at A would have had to wait for it to turn a profit. In fact, prices came close to stopping the trade out, once they nosedived to the signal at C. Many traders prefer entries such as C, but more often than not, you'll encounter ones at A.

This is why trading is so tough. You never know what the market will do next. All you can do is enter on the basis of intelligent principles and hope for the best after that.

Two Bar Reversals

Two bar reversals can be thought of as being a deconstructed pin bar. The pattern involves two bars, with the second undoing the progress of the first completely, and in an equal and opposite manner. When you superimpose the second bar over the first, the result is a pin bar.

Figure 5 - Two Bar Reversals at A and B

Figure 5 illustrates two instances of two bar reversals at A and B. Both of these reversals are bullish. You can see how the second bar reverses the first one entirely and is almost a mirror image of it. Once you superimpose the bar on the right over the bar on the left, you'll end up with a pin bar.

Two   bar   reversals   are   a

                                                                        r

eversal pattern. However, they're best traded as continuations of the larger trend, much like pins are traded. If you happen to spot an exceptionally large two bar reversal at the end of a trend, then you can trade this as a reversal.

For the most part, you should look for them to form in the same areas where pins are formed within a trend. This means the tiny sideways movements that occur in a trend are the ideal spots for them to form.

These patterns are harder to spot, and you won't find them very often on a chart. However, when you do find them, you're assured of lesser competition, and as a result, they'll work out more often. Notice the forceful nature with which price rises after the reversal at B. This is how a lot of reversals play themselves out.

This brings our look at candlestick price patterns, to a close. Remember to focus on the underlying order flow characteristics instead of looking at the geometrical shape of the pattern. Geometry doesn't equal intelligent trading. It'll only cause you to lose money.

Instead, focus on the order flow characteristics and what this is communicating to you.

Chapter 4:

Trends and Ranges

I've been talking up trends and ranges quite a bit, and now you've finally arrived at the place where you'll learn all about them! Trends and ranges are, at once, both simple and complex. The simple version doesn't require me to spend more than a few lines describing them.

If you open a chart and see prices moving upwards from bottom left to top right or from top left to bottom right, that's a trend. If it's moving sideways, it's a range. That sounds simple enough, but in practice it's quite different. What catches out most traders is that trends can have ranges within them, and that ranges serve as transition points between two opposite trends.

A lot of price action in the market can be unlocked by simply looking at the ranges that are being formed. This is where we'll begin.

Ranges

There are two kinds of ranges that are typically formed. Some traders might argue there are three, but this is a matter of semantics. At the end of the day, you'll see ranges that are formed within trends and those that are formed at the end of a trend. These two types of ranges are very different from one another, in terms of structure and behavior.

Ranges in the middle of trends tend to be short and don't feature too much countertrend movement. Counter trend refers to the direction opposite to the existing trend. If the trend is bearish, the bulls are working countertrend.

Ranges formed at the end of trends are much larger and witness multiple swings in price within them. In fact, some of these ranges last for years on end, and can contain mini trends within them thanks to their size.

So, why do these ranges exhibit such characteristics? To understand this, we need to take a step back and look at how order flow proceeds in the market. Every trend is born within a range. Let's take the example of a bull trend that starts from a range at the end of a bear trend.

The trend initially begins from the latter half of the large range. Here, bulls begin to overcome the bears slowly and eventually break out upwards. Initially, the bulls are quite strong, since they've managed to absorb all bearish pressure, as they built their strength within the range.

Occasionally during these times, the bulls will take a breather. This is when you'll see short and small sideways movements. In the earlier portions of trends, these ranges might be just a few bars long. These ranges are where you'll see inside bars and pin bars form, for the most part.

These ranges offer the trader a great way to enter in the direction of the trend. As prices exit these short ranges, and as the bulls continue to push prices upwards, even more bulls join the party. However, as prices continue to rise, the bears come back into play. At higher price levels, there are more bears waiting, and they begin to exert their influence on prices.

The result is more ranges. The size of the range depends on the level of bearish participation in the market. The more bearish (countertrend) participation there is, the larger the range will be.

As trends progress, you'll see the size of the sideways movements within them increase. The more bears there are present, the more time the bulls need to overcome them. The result is a sideways move that lasts longer. As prices move higher, the bearish participation increases.

At this point, the bulls are steadily losing control of the market, even if they have the dominant position for now. They make one last push upwards, and this results in a huge bullish bar. This is called a buying climax and is accompanied by huge volumes. In the stock markets, you can identify climaxes quite easily, thanks to volumes being available.

In FX, it isn't as straightforward. You'll need to compare the size of the potential climax bar to the rest and see how it matches up. The climax results in bulls overextending themselves, and it is at this stage that the bears spot an opportunity to quickly do some damage.

They reassert themselves in the market, and you'll likely see a large two bar reversal or an engulfing bar pattern form. Prices bounce downwards. However, the bulls haven't disappeared entirely. They're still present at lower levels and try their best to keep pushing prices up.

However, the bears have got a taste of what it's like to be in control, and they're unlikely to let go of it. The result is a balanced environment where neither side has full control. Therefore, prices move sideways in a large range, as the order flow is redistributed between bulls and bears.

Ranges that occur at the end of bullish trends are called distributive. This is because orders are being sold for the most part. The bulls, who were present from the beginning, are not selling their holdings; they recognize the signs of exhaustion that the climax indicates.

The bears, for their part, also recognize this. The only people who don't recognize this are the dumb money traders who still believe in the myth of an ever rising market. They keep buying, and the intelligent bears are now selling them all the stock or units they need.

Soon prices will tumble downwards, and these traders will lose money. At some point in this large range, the bears decide that enough is enough, and they begin to depress prices. The same cycle begins all over again, but this time in the bearish direction.

Let's look at an example to see how this works in the market.

TSLA (Tesla)

Everyone loves TSLA, so let's take a look at how this cycle played out in the stock, starting from December 2019 onwards. The chart I'll be focusing on is the 60-minute.

Figure 6 - TSLA 60 H1

Overall, you can clearly see that the stock was on a bullish run, from December onwards. The bars at the bottom of the chart indicate volumes. Usually, when trading stocks, you want to pay attention to the volumes as well, since this is important data. However, it isn't as if volumes can make or break your trade decisions.

In order to help you understand how you can use the same techniques in FX, I'll ignore the volumes in this example. Instead, I will highlight important points where volumes can offer additional insight as we move forward.

The ranges in this chart have been marked with numbers from one to six. Ranges 3 and 4 could technically be clubbed into one big range, but this is subjective. It isn't as important for you to figure out the exact boundaries of the range, as it is to understand order flow.

Ranges 1 and 2 are still within the larger end of trend range that extends to the left of the chart. For space purposes, I haven't shown this, since it is a pretty large one. However, this is where the trend begins. It isn't particularly strong, but you can see how the bulls push prices up with much bearish resistance.

The ranges are evidence of this. Notice that the bars in them are smaller, on average, and the prices move sideways or with an upward tilt, as opposed to moving back down. This indicates the bulls are in control.

Range 3 also plays out the same way, and following this, we see price gap up strongly, and then it promptly settles into range 4. This is where the bears first make their voices heard. From the end of 3, until the end of 4, notice how price has moved sideways. This is also the first time that strong bearish bars have been printed.

Previously, all bearish bars were swiftly repulsed, but the one in range 4 takes some time to be undone. This should give us pause, and indicates that the bears might not be strong yet, but they're certainly going to have a say in things as prices move higher.

Following another gap up, we have range 5. This is a lot like ranges 1-3, but don't be fooled into thinking that the bears have packed up. Perhaps they didn't wish to participate at these levels, who knows? The presence of a single, small range doesn't negate the previous bearish bars we saw in range 4.

As prices move higher and settle into range 6, we see the bears come out to play. Notice how the upward push is negated. This is the first time that bullish gains have been forcefully erased. Clearly, the bears are getting stronger. As this chart ends, our view is that the bulls are still in control but the bears are getting stronger.

We should expect to see longer ranges and prices moving back deeper into the trend as it progresses. We don't know how much longer the trend will last. It's safe to say that there is still some way to go. If we spot any entry opportunities in the ranges that form, going long on them is the right move.

If we've already entered any positions, we keep holding on to them. There's no point in exiting, since clearly, the trend has a ways to go.

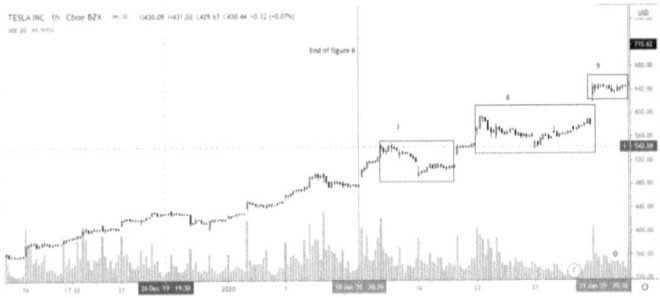

Figure 7 - TSLA H1 Continued

Figure 7 shows what happens next. The vertical line in the middle indicates the end of Figure 6 and was where we left things previously. We see the price gap up and then move into range 7.

7 is an interesting range. Here, prices move actively in a countertrend fashion, as we expected at the end of figure 6. It retraces the bullish gain quite a lot until the bulls step back in. Clearly, the bulls are weakening. If the bulls were strong, the bears wouldn't be able to push back this strongly into the trend.

Price gaps bullishly and moves higher, and we then see range 8. This is comfortably the largest range we've seen thus far, and is in line with our expectations following the bearish presence we've seen so far. The bars within it are small, there's some countertrend movement, but bullish pressure is low as well.

There's another bullish gap and an immediate sideways movement. Something to notice is the large number of gaps we're witnessing. All of these gaps are occurring at the open. Prices are not moving upwards intraday. The pattern, over the last few sessions we've seen, is that price gaps up and then hovers around that level for the most part.

In short, bullish moves are happening due to overnight pressure. There are very few bulls present during market hours, and the bears have free rein. It's safe to say that this kind of bullish behavior indicates that the smarter bulls have exited or are planning on exiting. It is the dumb money buying TSLA that is causing such abrupt move upwards.

Given that bearish pressure has increased even more during this time, we should expect larger ranges, and even countertrend moves. At this point, it would be wise to bring the stops on earlier positions, and close or even cash in on the profit they've made. After all, the bears might assert themselves soon.

Entering new long positions is unwise, but we can't say this for sure. When in doubt, it pays to be an aggressive trader as opposed to a conservative one. Therefore, we'll still take entry opportunities, but given that the market might not run for a lot longer, a tighter stop and closer reward levels are in order.

Don't worry about stop placement and reward levels just yet. You'll learn about these in the next few chapters. For now, just focus on understanding how ranges help you figure out which stage the trend is in.

Figure 8 - TSLA H1 Continued

Figure 8 illustrates how this bull trend ended in TSLA. The vertical line on the left indicates where we left off in Figure 7. Range 9 is marked as well. Price once again gaps up, and the bulls manage to push higher during the day. This is a bit odd and goes against what we've seen thus far.

The size of the bullish bars have also increased a lot more. This is even more odd. It indicates one of two things has happened. Either the bears have decided to collectively disappear and leave the bulls without any opposition or the bulls are expending a lot of effort to overcome the bears.

The former situation is unlikely to happen. The latter makes more sense. In short, we're building up to a buying climax. Since this is a stock, pay attention to the volume bars at the bottom. Notice how they're much larger in size compared to the ones to their left.

This indicates the bulls are pouring in tons of resources and buying up TSLA stock, in a bid to push prices higher. The next day, price gaps up even more, and immediately we see a bearish bar with a large wick and a large tail. Again, notice how volume jumps up. This is a clear signal of a buying climax.

Volumes have exploded, bar ranges have increased with them but prices haven't gone up. The gap here is monstrous. TSLA gapped over $100 overnight! Dumb money has fully entered the stock, and it's time to get out.

If TSLA were an FX market instrument, you wouldn't have had the confirmation of a climax that volumes would have provided. The intelligent play here would have been to move stops close and then wait for some sort of bearish signal. Notice the angle of attack that price has adopted. It's almost vertical.

This is clearly unsustainable, and given the explosion in bar size, you can be almost 100% sure that a climax is playing itself out. Right at the end of the day, we see a bearish engulfing bar form. Geometrical purists will claim that this is not an engulfer but from an order flow perspective; but it most definitely is an engulfer.

Notice that the close of this bar is close to the day's open. It is here that the intelligent FX trader will exit. Subsequent price action shows that this would have been the right choice. TSLA moves into a large range where orders are being redistributed. It makes it back up to the highs it made down the road, but bearish gaps come to dominate as the stock begins to tumble.

Notice that throughout all of this, I didn't make any mention of Elon Musk's sometimes deranged tweets or of public sentiment. Considering that this chart tracks the last half of December through February 2020, it's quite an achievement that we haven't paid any attention to the coronavirus either.

TSLA's movements were there for everyone to see if they could read the nature of the ranges being printed. This method works no matter what the instrument is or what is going on in the world. On the surface of it, the Covid-19 lockdown prompted the selloff in TSLA.

However, the conditions for the selloff were already present before the lockdowns hit. Traders would have been seeking to sell even before the news became public, just by looking at the charts.

Trends

Range analysis will give you deep insight into the way the market works and how trends progress. Truth be told, a lot of range analysis involves looking at trends. After all, ranges are a part of the trend.

When it comes to the portion of the trend that is outside the ranges, your primary task is to evaluate the speed and angle with which price is moving ahead. The extent of the moves in the direction of the trend, and the volumes with which they move ahead are crucial to evaluate.

As you've already seen in the case of TSLA, if you spot a trend that is progressing, primarily thanks to gaps, then this is a fairly good indicator of the smart money having long since pulled out. Stock markets are a bit easier to trade in this sense. They have defined opening and closing hours and, as a result, these gaps form.

They allow you to quickly spot how the market is progressing. The always-on nature of the FX market makes it tough for such gaps to form. However, you should pay attention to the extent of the moves, as well as the angle with which the trend progresses. A shallow angle means a weak trend.

An extremely steep angle can mean multiple things, depending on which portion of the trend you're looking at. If a steep angle occurs during the initial portion of the trend, it's a strong signal for you to buckle up for the long haul. This indicates that the trending forces are strong and it's going to be a while before the trend ends.

This doesn't mean you should be careless. As you'll learn in the next chapter, sometimes the strongest of trends can hit a brick wall and turn the other way.

A steep angle towards the end of a trend, after the countertrend forces have long since established themselves, indicates the possibility of a climax. Obviously, as you've just learned, you should not be taking positions in such an environment. If you caught the trend in the earlier stages, you should be preparing to exit your positions. You could even wait for the trend to exhaust itself, and trade the other direction if you spot an engulfer or a large two bar reversal.

In terms of size, you will see the largest bars towards the climax phase. Many traders confuse pure size for strength. This is not the case. Climactic price action usually results in large price bars printing, but these lack any sort of backup. Typically, the climax will build up and result in one large, or a couple of large bars, printing in the direction of the trend.

In contrast, real strength is when the trending forces make significant gains without overextending themselves. During the beginning of the trend, you will see price bars print that are big in size, but not outlandishly large. They will have long bodies and few wicks or tails. They will also be large in number.

You won't see one or two bars print and then abruptly stop. A good way to further evaluate the strength of the trend, at that point, is to look at the accompanying ranges. If the ranges are small, the trend is strong. If they've been getting progressively bigger, then it doesn't matter what the trending bars tell you, pay attention to the ranges.

As you can see, the markets can be a confounding place. In order to trade trends well, you need to read ranges. The question is: How do you enter your orders, and where should you be placing your stop loss and take profit levels?

How to Trade Trends

There are two approaches you can use to trade the markets. The first is to trade unassisted, and the other is assisted. Assisted refers to the use of a price action pattern or an indicator to help you decide where your order needs to be placed. It also helps you receive some degree of confirmation that your analysis is right.

Confirmation is a tricky thing. You always want the market to back-up your analysis in some way, but many traders take this to an extreme. They begin to confuse confirmation with certainty. They don't trust themselves or understand that there is no such thing as a 100% certain method, when it comes to the markets.

This is why trading unassisted is so tough for most traders. Yet, this is how professional traders trade the markets. They use indicators and patterns, but they don't build entire trading systems around them. They use them as supplements at best. You can trade profitably in the short term with assistance, but over the long run you should make the switch to trading unassisted.

If you're trading with an indicator, the indicator itself will give you the entry signal. You can place your order at the market, with a stop beyond a suitable support or resistance level. You'll learn more about support and resistance in the next chapter. In terms of exits, you can either exit based on where the indicator tells you to exit, or you can exit at a predetermined multiple, based on your risk management metrics.

When using candlestick patterns, your analysis will begin with the range/trend analysis of the sort you've just learned. Look for patterns in ranges. Once you spot them, enter on the close of the final bar of the relevant pattern. Place a stop beyond either the cluster of bars or beyond a support/resistance level.

- Inside bars - Enter on stop beyond the break of the largest bar. Stop placed below or above the smaller bar.
- Pin bar - Enter at market on close of the pin bar. Stop below or above the tail or wick respectively.
- Engulfing bar - Enter at market on close of the outside bar. Stop at 50% of the larger bar or beyond it.
- Two bar reversal - Enter at market on close of the second bar. Stop at 50% of the two bars if they're large or beyond the bars if they're small.

If you choose to trade unassisted, then the best way to enter is either on a limit or at market. Your stop will be placed beyond the closest relevant support or resistance level. Here's how it usually works. Let's say you were tracking TSLA's uptrend as we've seen in this chapter.

If TSLA was moving through a small range, you could enter anywhere in that range at market, and place your stop loss above the resistance level of that range. The resistance refers to the upper boundary of the range.

If you're someone who is nitpicky about getting their entry price spot on, you could set a limit at the top of the range, and wait for the market to fill your order with the stop loss placed beyond the resistance level.

In the first case, you're guaranteed to get in on the trend, while in the second, you're going to have to wait and possibly even miss the trend at that point. The best way to handle this is to enter at market in the earlier portions of the trend, and use limits in the latter half of the trend, where you don't want to get in unless you absolutely have to.

You will be playing around with both of these methods when you implement my seven steps, as I'll detail them later, so don't worry about figuring this out right now. I'll be giving you a framework that will help you figure out which method of trading is best suited for your needs in those seven steps.

For now, let's take a look at support and resistance and see how these will help you trade better.

Chapter 5:

Support and Resistance

If you've dabbled in trading before, you probably think you know all about support and resistance. This topic is something that is both simple and complex at the same time. It's simple in that spotting these levels is something that, even someone who doesn't know anything about trading, can do.

They're complex because spotting levels is one thing, and trading them successfully is entirely another. This is because the support and resistance (sr) levels you should be paying attention to, depend on the stage of the trend you're in. The deeper you go into a trend, the stronger you want your relevant sr levels to be.

In the large end of trend ranges, there are just two levels you will pay attention to. These also happen to be the strongest kinds of sr levels you will ever see on a chart. These are the boundaries of the range. Given that these are the strongest, it makes sense to look at these first.

Range Boundaries

Sr levels acquire relevance because traders tend to remember the important price zones in a chart. In other words, if the price has bounced from $101 in the past, multiple times, you can bet that it will again have a decent bounce in the future.

How much of a bounce will occur, depends on the strength of the existing trend, as well as the strength of the level itself. Levels that were weak in the past will not witness much of a bounce, while strong ones will provoke some reaction. What happens with such levels is that traders lie in wait as price approaches them.

As price hits these levels, traders place their orders and, as a result, prices bounce off them. The boundaries of large ranges are especially important because this is where order flow is most clear. At the top of the range, everyone knows the bears are in charge. At the bottom, it is the bulls. In between, who knows?

Remember that ranges at the end of a trend witness massive redistribution of order strength. This means that the middle of these ranges are full of traders shuffling their orders around. In the case of our TSLA example, the bears are trying to sell TSLA at the highest level possible, since this is where they'll make the most profit.

The bulls have recognized that they aren't all that strong anymore, and retreat to lower levels where they can amass more strength to assault the bears at higher levels. Thus, the boundaries of the range are formed and clear lines in the sand are drawn.

In the middle, we have either clueless traders who don't understand what is going on, or sophisticated traders who are pushing bids and offers trying to gauge what the market is doing. Either way, it is no place for a small trader. In TSLA's case, the bottom boundary broke and the bears asserted themselves strongly.

Since the bottom boundary was such an important level, breaking it is significant. Once it's broken, it isn't as if the market simply forgets it. Instead, that broken strong support turns into strong resistance from where traders short TSLA. Why does this happen?

Put simply, there are many traders who aren't fanatical bulls or bears. They simply go with the path of least resistance. If a strong support level is broken, they decide that it's pretty much curtains for the bull market, and they side with the bears, thereby accelerating the downswing.

This results in the boundaries of these large ranges having memories, so to speak. Traders will always look to place orders from them. If you're trading a large range, then stick to the boundaries and trade both directions until one of them is broken, or if there is a clear indication that a strong trend is beginning.

Repeatedly Tested Levels

One notch below, in terms of strength, are levels that are repeatedly tested by price. These are the areas where price bounces from, over and over again. As price approaches these levels, you can bet that another bounce will occur.

Large range boundaries will often exhibit this kind of behavior, but it occurs within smaller ranges as well. If you're trading smaller ranges, then stick to the direction of the trend instead of trading both sides of the market because smaller ranges indicate that the trend is still firmly in place.

Your job is to trade with it as much as possible. When these repeatedly tested levels are broken, you will often see prices hit them from the other side before progressing in the direction of the trend.

Figure 9 - Repeatedly Tested Levels

Figure 9 is an illustration of these kinds of levels. In this case, we have a range that is broken, after which price accelerates into a bear trend. Notice how price bounces off the bottom of the range at 1 and 2 in the chart. Price gaps below this level but still rushes up to retest it from below before descending.

When looking at such levels, examining the nature of the bounces is instructive. In this case, the bounce at 1 was strong. Notice the angle with which price bounced back up and also the extent to which it went up after the bounce. Now compare this to the rather anemic bounce at 2.

Price moves sideways above it and barely bounces up. As a trade, you would have been justified in going long at 2. However, once your trade went for a loss, your next step should have been to short the level at 2 and ride the strong downtrend to massive profits. This is how smart traders play the market.

Keep in mind that, this course of action depends on your range/trend analysis holding up. Don't take this to mean that you should go ahead and short or go long on every single repeatedly tested level in sight. Discretion is necessary, and you should build the range/trend picture first before paying attention to the levels.

Why don't I zoom out a bit on Figure 9 to see if the overall context would have changed the actions I mentioned just now?

Figure 10: TSLA Levels

Figure 10 is a zoomed out version of Figure 9, and we're still looking at TSLA. As a matter of fact, we're looking at the bear trend that develops after the bull trend ends in the previous chapter.

The bounces from Figure 9 at 1,2 and 3, are clearly marked along with the level. However, notice that just above this level, there also exists the much stronger range boundary that occurs after the bull trend exhausts itself. This is indicated by the letter A and is a zone.

The potential trades from this zone have been indicated with boxes. Notice that you have three long and one short opportunity. Of the three long trades, two go for a loss. After the final long goes for a loss, the range boundary is broken, and now you need to go short, which has also been indicated by a box.

This means you're shorting right into the level indicated in Figure 9. It doesn't matter though, since you're shorting from a much stronger level, and as a result, the level indicated in Figure 9 (and in Figure 10 as a single horizontal line) doesn't matter. It isn't relevant.

Much like with candlestick patterns, you need to evaluate the overall price action before deciding which levels are relevant. If you didn't do this beforehand, you might have blindly bought 1 and 2 without realizing you're trading right against a strong bear trend.

This is why so many traders lose money. They apply sr and price patterns in a formulaic way, without looking at the bigger picture. The short entry at 3 is justified because it is with the trend. However, going long at 1 and 2 is not justified at all since you're going countertrend right where the new trend is at its strongest.

Swing Points

Swing points also function as sr, and these are the most common type of sr you will see on a chart. They also happen to be the most tricky ones to trade because the strength with which price approaches them can be difficult to gauge.

When broken, swing points often behave as sr in the other direction, much like the previous two levels you learned about. However, this isn't always the case. If the trend is strong, then you can expect the price to retest the broken swing point before continuing on its way.

However, if the trend is too strong, price will likely never retest it. If the trend is too weak, it will probably breach the level and hang around near it for a while. Generally speaking, you want to match the strength of the trend you're in with the strength of the swing point level you're looking at.

To better understand this, let's take a look at Figure 10 once more. Pay attention to the price wing at the bottom right-hand corner of the chart. This is a swing point, and price eventually breaks down past it.

If prices were to retest this level from the bottom, would you short this level? To answer this question, we need to take a step back and look at the range/trend scenario at play here.

We'll begin by looking at the ranges currently present on the chart. Price has just broken out of a large range. If we consider this bearish trend to have begun from the top of that range, we can see that so far, the ranges have been either long or medium-sized. The one just before the bottom range boundary breaks is pretty big, but this is understandable.

This isn't evidence of bullish strength. If anything, it shows that the bears were strong enough to force the trend. What about the ranges after this large range breaks? We have just one clear example that is just below the big range's broken boundary.

Notice that the move down was a gap and recall what you learned about them. While a single gap by itself isn't a sign of poor quality trading, it is something to take a note of. Alarmingly, the next leg down after this small range is also a gap.

This tells us that the selling quality is probably low and that despite the bearish nature of this market, the trend isn't very strong in TSLA. In all probability, the slightest show of bullish strength will cause it to move into an accumulative range, which is the type of range that forms at the end of a bear trend. In these ranges, buyers look to absorb all selling pressure and 'accumulate' the stock.

We have three strong bearish bars that produce this swing point. This is encouraging, but notice that these are the only strong bearish bars that have been produced in succession since the trend broke out of the large range on top.

There are two ways of looking at this: Either the high-quality bears are now ready to jump in, or these three bars are an exception. Given everything that has transpired before in this trend, with the low quality of selling and high number of gaps, it would be wise to lean towards the second option.

As a result, we should look to stay away from shorting this swing point if price retests it from the bottom. As it turns out, price gapped down below once more and retested this level to swing lower. However, it quickly rose back up and moved into an accumulative range. Figure 11 illustrates this.

Figure 11: TSLA End of the Bear Trend

As you can see on the left-hand side of this chart, price retests our swing low in question, indicated by the circle. It does fall a lot further. Our approach, as detailed in the previous paragraph, would have caused us to miss this fall. We would have held on to our previous shorts and would have exited at the slightest sign of bullish strength.

This means the large bullish bar that occurs after the low is formed in this chart, would have been our cue to exit. If you look at the distance between the level of our 'missed' trade entry to the close of this strong bullish bar, you can see that there isn't much distance at all. Therefore, there isn't too much opportunity cost involved here.

A novice trader or a losing one would have wanted to capture every single downswing in that trend. This is not a realistic way to trade. You will never capture the full extent of a swing. Instead, you need to look for evidence that indicates it's time to get out and take your exit when the market gives it to you.

You might miss a few trades like the one above, and it will seem as if you've sat out a good, profitable swing. However, in the long run you'll save yourself money and commission costs by trading this way. As you can see in the example above, there really wasn't much of a profit to be had by trading that swing point.

Still, it illustrates how tough it can be to get swing points right. Whether there was any profit to be had or not, price did retest it, and price did fall from it. This was something we did not predict in our analysis.

The market works on the basis of probabilities, and not every decision you make is going to be successful. You will have moments such as this, where you'll make a decision and see that the market does something else. This is perfectly fine. As you'll learn in the chapter on risk management, trading isn't about being right or correctly predicting the market's path.

It's about figuring out your odds and aligning yourself to them accordingly. You don't even need to be right most of the time, in order to make money. If that sentence doesn't make any sense to you, then you need to spend some time understanding how trading risk management works.

Chapter 6:

Fundamental Analysis

In this chapter, we're going to leave the world of charting behind and dive into the financials of companies. Don't worry, you won't need an accounting degree to be able to figure out what's going on with a company.

Fundamental analysis, when used to trade stocks, is a lot different than the type of analysis that is used to figure out which stocks to hold for the long term. Truth be told, you will need to carry out the technical analysis that you've learned all about this far in this book.

The role that fundamentals will play is to help you figure out which stocks are ripe for trading, and which ones are better left well alone. I must also mention that carrying out fundamental analysis when it comes to FX, will make your head spin, and you don't have to do it.

It's far easier to carry this out with stocks because ultimately, all the fundamental metrics depend on a company's prospects and on its financials. In contrast, there are tons of macroeconomic factors that drive the price of a currency pair. There is just one fundamental factor that you can employ when it comes to FX, and that is correlation. I'll talk about this later in this chapter.

As of now, let's stick with stocks. The place to begin is trading volumes. You want the stocks you're operating in to be well traded, or liquid. Stay away from stocks that witness less than 100,000 shares traded, on average, during a session. This will ensure enough liquidity should you need to enter or exit quickly. It will also prevent you from being gouged when you wish to exit profitable trades.

Next, pay attention to the VIX. The VIX is the volatility index in the market. The higher the volatility is, the more careful you should be. When volatility is high, you want to place your stops further away from your entries, to account for gyrations in price.

High levels in the VIX aren't a reason for you to stay away from the markets entirely. It's just that you should take note of these levels and adjust your trading accordingly. Once you've noted the VIX's levels, you need to look at the overall trend of the market. This can be done by looking at the way the S&P 500 is behaving.

If you notice a bullish trend, it's best to confine yourself to sectors that are even more bullish than the overall market. Similarly, sectors that are more bearish than the overall

market, are good places to operate in bear markets. You can gauge the relative bullishness or bearishness of the sectors by comparing sector indices to the overall market index.

Make a list of the sectors that are stronger and weaker than the overall market. Then drill down into those sectors to identify the strongest amongst the strong sectors and the weakest in the weakest sectors. This way, you'll be able to capture a greater portion of moves in any direction.

Here's why this tactic is so powerful: In a bear market, all sectors and stocks fall. Even the strong ones. In such situations, you want to be siding with the stocks that are the weakest since these will fall far more than the ones that are strong.

Similarly, in bull markets, all sectors will experience a rise. Even the weak ones. By operating in the strong stocks, you'll gain a lot more than what you stand to make by going long in weaker stocks.

Keep in mind that you still need to carry out your technical analysis before deciding to place trades. The mere presence of relative strength isn't enough for you to decide to go long in anything.

One way of determining how volatile a stock will be is to look at a few financial ratios. Your broker will provide you with these ratios, so they aren't too hard to find.

Ratios

The point behind seeking out highly volatile stocks is to figure out how far a stock will move. As a trader you want to stick to stocks that are volatile in the sense where they move in a single direction with great force, as opposed to jumping up and down violently.

The stocks that do this tend to have highly leveraged balance sheets. Leverage here refers to the amount of debt they're carrying relative to their equity. Equity is simply a measure of how much of the company is owned by the shareholders. A company with a 60/40 debt to equity ratio is highly leveraged.

It's a lot like you borrowing $60 and placing $40 of your own money to buy a stock worth $100. If the price of this stock rises by 50% to $150, you've just made a 125% return. If your trading operations had a stock ticker attached to it, imagine it zooming up 125%!

However, if it dropped by 50% to $50, you would be wiped out. Imagine your stock dropping to zero steeply. The same thing happens with companies as well. The greater their debt, the more volatile their stock is. When good news occurs, their stock prices go rocketing upwards. During bad times they dive down with high velocity.

If your broker doesn't display the debt to equity ratio, then you can calculate this from the company's balance sheet. Look at the total debt figure in the balance sheet. Divide this number by the number listed under the shareholders' equity line item. A company that has a ratio greater than one is considered highly leveraged.

Goodwill

Goodwill is an accounting creation; I'm not going to spend time discussing why it makes sense. As such, it is not a financial item such as cash or revenues. If company A decides to buy company B, it usually has to pay a value that is in excess of what that company is worth. This is to make the offer enticing.

The difference between company B's value and the price paid for it is recorded as goodwill on the balance sheet. Companies with a large amount of goodwill usually run into trouble at some point. This is because they're highly reliant on acquisitions to grow their business.

Acquisitions are tough to assess. Often the company that is acquired turns out to be a dud and this leads to the buying company writing down their investment in it. The accounting term for this is called an impairment. Watch out for this term in the news. You can even add a Google alert for it.

A company that has been taking a raft of impairments is on weak ground and if its technicals hold up, it might provide great opportunities.

Special Situations

Speaking of alerts, setting them up for terms such as 'lawsuit' or 'settled' or 'settlement' is also a good idea. Special situations such as these tend to cause huge volatility, the good sort, in the stocks that are affected by the decision. While swing trading isn't the best strategy to deploy in these conditions, you can wait for the volatility to spike and then use the methods mentioned earlier to get in on the trend.

Another special situation to watch out for is spinoffs. A spinoff occurs when a company decides to carve out a department of its own into a separate company. There are many reasons for doing this. Perhaps the division would be more profitable by itself. Perhaps by divesting it, the parent company can shore up its own finances.

Spinoffs tend to do well over the long term and buy and hold investors love them. However, once the spinoff is live, you can expect some bullishness in the stock.

What Not to Do

Many traders try to trade the news. They read about trade wars and hop onto the 5G bandwagon thinking it'll be affected. The fact is that news disseminates instantly these days. If you're reading it, it's already too late. Someone has already got there ahead of you and the market has priced this into the stock.

The only exception is in regard to major announcements such as lawsuits that are scheduled to be released at a certain point. These announcements are covered under insider trading laws and therefore, everyone receives them at the same time. Despite this, you should stay away from trading the event itself.

Instead, look at the trend that is formed after the news item is released and you'll be able to get in on it.

Inverse and Leveraged ETFs

ETF stands for exchange traded fund. These can be thought of as being hedge funds for the ordinary guy. They can have any type of strategy and are traded like common stock in the market. Most ETFs tend to track an underlying stock index and are safe investment vehicles.

There are some ETFs that are speculative vehicles. These are usually termed inverse ETFs. An inverse ETF moves in the opposite direction from its underlying index. For example, an inverse ETF tracking the S&P 500 will move up if the index falls and move down if the index rises.

There are also leveraged ETFs. These are appended by the term 2X or Double. A 2X ETF moves twice the distance of its underlying index. A 2X ETF on the S&P 500 will move 10 points if the index moves five points.

Finally, you can have inverse, 2X ETFs. These move twice the distance in the opposite direction from the underlying. Remember that it's best to go long on these ETFs instead of shorting them. They're a lot like calls and puts on their underlying index. Instead of shorting options, you would simply buy a particular type of option.

It's the same with these ETFs.

Correlation

The FX market offers huge opportunities when it comes to correlation. Truth be told, correlation used to offer massive plays in the market but these days, one-to-one opportunities are rare. This doesn't mean these plays don't exist. It's just that you'll need to get a little more creative with them.

For example, a popular correlation trade used to be gold and silver. These instruments (along with their CFDs) move at certain ratios. Traders look at the gold to silver ratio and if this value moves past a certain number, they use strategies that will result in the ratio converging at a certain value.

Trading this way is extremely complicated and the beginner is best served by standing aside. Instead, look for simpler correlation opportunities. One of the simplest correlations out there is the price of the USDCAD and the price of oil.

Canada's primary export is oil and price fluctuations in the commodity cause fluctuations in the currency pair as well. The relationship isn't one to one. You'll have to dig deeper to figure out what's going on. However, it is a simple relationship to understand, for the most part.

Similarly, the AUDUSD is dependent on the state of the Chinese economy. Anything that happens with China affects the Australian economy thanks to China being Australia's biggest customer.

Another phenomenon you can take advantage of is the currency peg. Many countries in the world peg their currency to the U.S. Dollar or the Euro. A good example of this is the Hong Kong Dollar. The HKD is pegged to the USD and as the HKDs price comes close to this peg, it automatically jumps up.

Brokers are aware of the peg, and you won't be able to take huge advantage of this, thanks to the spreads widening. However, you can speculate on the Hang Seng Index CFD. The Hang Seng is Hong Kong's stock market index. If the HKD rises in value, it tends to depress the earnings of HK companies. This causes drops in the index. I'm not talking about catastrophic drops, but they're enough for an intelligent trader to take advantage of.

Gold is correlated to fear. It sounds odd to read that statement but whenever turmoil hits the world's economy, gold jumps in price. As an asset it doesn't provide the investor with much but it receives huge demand from India and China whose economies are a lot less stable.

Gold is seen as a stable refuge in troubled times. When something unexpected happens, gold tends to jump in value. For example, when Donald Trump was elected President, gold jumped in value massively because no one knew what to expect or had even considered the possibility that a reality TV star could end up governing the most powerful country in the world.

Currently, the world's central banks are busy printing money to pay for bad assets. This is causing the value of currencies worldwide to decline. As a result, gold's price has been increasing massively over the past decade since it is seen as something that isn't going to depreciate.

Even if the world's economy collapsed, a person with gold could get by. This is not the case with cash that might prove to be worthless.

Chapter 7:

Technical Analysis

There are two parts to technical analysis. One is the bit that you learned earlier in this book, about trends/ranges and sr. The second part has to do with indicators. I'll say this right now: Trading with indicators is a losing proposition for most traders. Here's why.

Indicators are supposed to do what their name says. They indicate. They're not meant to form definitive conclusions with. Traders who rely on indicators as the pillars of their systems risk their indicators becoming obsolete. This happens all the time in the market.

The indicator craze has led to even more sophisticated indicators being developed. There are a few advanced indicators that use differential calculus to figure out market moves. This is a futile task to carry out. An indicator is once removed from price and twice removed from order flow.

Order flow, the buy and sell orders that traders place in the market, is what causes prices to fluctuate. Price charts reflect order flow and are the closest thing we have to it. Indicators are built on top of price charts and are thus deriving results from a derivation of order flow.

An indicator can therefore be as sophisticated as possible but at the end of the day, it will always lag because the data it is being fed is twice removed from the source. The best software and the most sophisticated calculations cannot overcome bad data.

Having said that, indicators can be wonderful supplements to your trading strategy. They can also be great ways for beginners to confirm that they're doing the right thing and seeing things correctly. Just keep in mind that all indicators lag and as a result, you're not going to be able to predict the market's direction.

You'll be able to confirm what has just happened or what is happening right now. Trend/range analysis and sr levels will help you figure out what is likely to happen over the short term. Not indicators.

DeMarker Indicator

The DeMarker indicator or DeM as it's called is an oscillator that is particularly effective when it comes to figuring out current market movement. Most technical analysis indicators fall into two categories. They're either trend indicators or oscillators.

An oscillator aims to measure market momentum. If price moves in a particular direction, how quickly does it move? A weak move indicates possible reversal sooner or later while strong moves tend to last for longer. Oscillators usually fluctuate in a band between zero and 100.

Whatever the maximum or minimum values might be, all oscillators move up and down within a fixed range. They also have overbought and oversold areas. An overbought area is one where price has risen too high and the oscillator indicates that a fall is due. An indicator moving into the oversold area means price is bound to rise shortly.

The DeM moves between 0 and 1, or between 0 and 0.1, depending on the settings on your trading software. The exact values aren't important. The overbought zone typically lies between 0.7 and one (0.07 and 0.1) and the oversold zone between 0.3 and one (0.03 and one).

Some sources claim that the DeM is a leading indicator. But this is nonsense. There isn't a single indicator on the planet that can predict the future. Such systems usually employ the DeM within convergence or divergence strategies.

This is when the trader looks at the indicator and compares its movement to price. If there is a divergence, if price moves faster than the indicator for example, then this means price is overextended and it must move in the opposite direction shortly.

Such strategies are extremely subjective and you're best served by staying away from them. They're used by traders who believe that indicators are the key to making profits. You've already learned why this thought is false.

The DeM, like all other oscillators, is best used in a ranging market. Do not use this in a trending market because the indicator will move into overbought or oversold levels and will remain there for a long time. Oscillators do not have the means to translate trending moves in the market.

In a range, prices fluctuate between one boundary and the other. This means, the trader can use an oscillator to accurately predict where price might turn or if a turn in the opposite direction is imminent.

You can also use oscillators in the latter stages of trends when the ranges are getting bigger and when countertrend moves are increasing. Another point to keep in mind with the DeM is that it is best used to trade in the direction of the trend, when you're using it prior to an end of trend range.

Figure 12: DeM Indicator

Figure 12 illustrates a situation in TSLA, which we've looked at before, here the trend transitions to a large range as it progresses towards its end. Notice how the DeM helps you get in on the trend early before it fully breaks out. The entry opportunities have been indicated by circles labeled one through seven.

Some of these will result in losses but overall, you'll end up making money. It's especially useful when the range in the second half of the chart develops. You can place your stop loss levels below the relevant support levels. In the case of trading in the range, this would be below the bottom boundary of the range.

Notice how all the trades are long. This is because that's what the trend direction is. If we were in a range that forms at the end of a trend, we would go short as well and sell everything the DeM dips below the overbought zone, indicated by the higher horizontal line in the indicator window.

Bollinger Bands

Bollinger Bands are neither trend indicators nor are they oscillators. Instead, they're literally price bands that exist on either side of the price candles. These bands are created on the basis of prior movements.

There are three lines to this indicator. A line in the middle that runs through the price bars is the moving average of the previous 20 bars' closing prices. The line on top is the upper band and this is three standard deviations from the mean (moving average). The line below, called the lower band, is also three standard deviations below the mean.

The idea behind this indicator is that if price moves beyond three sigma (standard deviations) from the mean, then a reversal is due. This is true in ranges where prices move in a somewhat predictable fashion. However, this is not the case in trends. Therefore, just like with the DeM, you should use bands only in ranges.

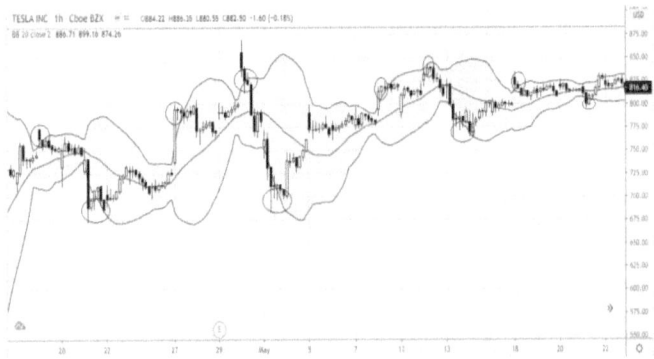

Figure 13: Bollinger Bands

Figure 13 illustrates the best way to trade Bollinger Bands. TSLA is in a choppy range that has an upward tilt. You could even consider this a large range within the uptrend. Whatever you classify it as, there's no doubt that price is choppy and it's a tough market to trade.

Every time price violates either the upper or lower band, we receive an indication to either go short or long respectively. If price peeks out above the upper band, notice how it immediately declines, more often than not. Similarly, every time it peeks out below the lower band, it invariably moves back up.

You can enter on the open of the violating bar or you can enter at its close. Alternatively, you could set a stop order on entry with the trigger being the band value. The stop loss should be placed beyond the band's extremity.

Exits in the case of Bollinger Bands are simple. You simply ride price back to the other end of the band and exit once it touches it or if you've hit a predetermined risk multiple (which you'll learn about in the next chapter).

Average Directional Index

The average directional index or ADX is a trend indicator and unlike the ones featured thus far, should be used only in trending portions. You can use them in the early stage ranges as well. However, as the trend progresses, the ADX loses its potency and will throw incorrect values.

The ADX is one of the oldest indicators developed in trading. There are many traders who claim that it's now useless since everyone uses it. This is untrue. What is true is that the indicator is used in wrong ways.

The indicator has three lines associated with it. There is the ADX line itself and two more lines called the +DI and -DI. These lines measure the bullish and bearish strength in the instrument respectively. The ADX line is simply an average of these two.

If the ADX prints values over 30, the instrument is considered to be in a strong trend. Anything below this is a weak or non-existent trend. While most traders use the indicator when the trend is well and truly on, the true power of the ADX lies in its ability to alert you to the formation of a new trend.

Trends begin in the large ranges that occur at the end of a previous trend. It can be tough to spot these moments. The ADX can alert you to when this occurs by printing values over 20 or 25.

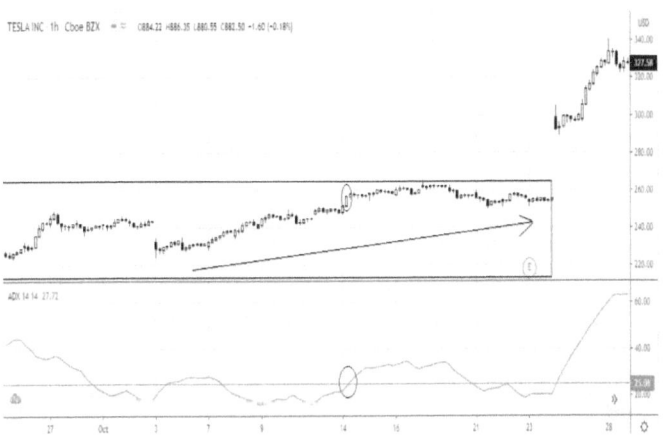

Figure 14 - ADX

Figure 14 shows TSLA in a large range before it breaks out to form a bullish trend. The top of the range had held since July 2019 (the chart shows October 2019). This is an H1 chart, so this is a pretty strong range.

For starters, notice how price moves gently upwards towards the top of the range. This by itself is a pretty good sign that the bulls are ready to break out. The ADX gives us notice of this phenomenon by printing a value above 25 and by staying there for a while before dipping back down.

By entering when it moved above 25, coupled with the rising price, you could have entered well in advance of the breakout and realized a huge profit once price gapped up. A few things for you to note in this example.

Do not be swayed by the fact that the ADX dipped below 25. This doesn't mean the trend suddenly disappeared. Remember, we're still in a large range. The ADX will eventually print incorrect values. The driver behind your long entry decision is the rising lows that price is forming.

You don't need to enter right when the ADX moves above 25. Instead, you could wait and watch for more evidence of higher lows and enter closer to the breakout.

The second thing to note is that unlike an oscillator, the ADX does not provide directional guidance. Whether the trend is bullish or bearish, it will print values and will rise accordingly as the trend gathers strength. Some traders use the DI lines to figure out direction.

You don't need the assistance of these lines at all. You can look at the price chart and use trend/range analysis to figure out what's going on. Note that in the scenario highlighted above, the DI lines won't do you much good. Since price is in a range, they'll simply crisscross one another and won't give you any worthy signals.

Instead, watch for price movement and for signs of price breaking out. The ADX will give you notice of this beforehand and you'll be able to take full advantage of this.

There are many indicators out there such as the MACD, RSI, Stochastic indicator and so on. All of these work in the same way as the ones I've highlighted. These three indicators cover a lot of ground when it comes to deciphering price movement. You have a trend indicator that helps you spot the start of a trend before it's fully blossomed.

You have an oscillator that helps you trade ranges. The Bollinger Bands will help you trade ranges and is a fully contained trading system by itself. Don't overcomplicate your trading by using indicators. This is what the average unsuccessful trader does. If you follow their actions, you're going to get their results.

Start off by using trend/range analysis techniques and then move forward from there.

Chapter 8:

Risk Management

This is perhaps the most important chapter in this book. The material here will help you figure out what the reality of trading is and what sort of mindset you need to carry with you when you're in the markets. Many people fail at trading despite having fantastic trading systems.

Why is this? It doesn't have to do with mindset, although that plays a role. What it really comes down to is risk management. Risk management is a skill that very few of us learn in life. The education system teaches us the exact opposite of what we need to learn in terms of real world risk.

I'll begin by having you carry out a small thought exercise. Think back to how many times in your life you've followed all the rules demanded by a task, perfectly. Now recollect how many times you've failed at a task despite doing everything correctly. The older you are, the more instances you'll have because the real world operates on very different terms than what we learn in school.

Lastly, think about how often you've witnessed people doing all the wrong things and still becoming successful. They are nowhere near as good as you or know as much about the subject, but still get ahead of you. Why does this happen? People who have bosses who are less than competent than they are wonder about this all the time.

Most people chalk it up to life being unfair and move on. As a trader, you can't do this unfortunately. By operating in the markets you're subject to the most random place on earth. You can do everything right and still lose money. Your indicator and analysis might indicate that a trend is imminent or that some level is strong enough to hold.

You're still likely to watch prices crash through them and you'll lose money. Unsuccessful traders thus put trading success down to luck and think of it as just gambling. Academics, who're sometimes as far divorced from reality as the sun is from the moon, write lengthy papers on how luck is what determines success in the market.

All of this reveals just how poorly the human mind is designed to understand risk. Perhaps designed is the wrong word. Our brains are remarkably adaptable. It's simply a case of having learned the wrong things.

All of us grow up in what can be thought of as being linear systems. Think back to how you advanced in school. You learned a bunch of information and sat for an exam. The more questions you answered correctly in the test, the higher your grade was. If your grade was high enough, you moved on to the next grade. This continued until you graduated from college.

Then you started working a job and continued to do the same things. You corrected your boss a few times by pointing out a few errors. You also corrected colleagues, thinking that they appreciated your honest feedback. Next thing you know, you've received an unfavorable review. The person who meanwhile schmoozes your boss gets promoted, despite them having less than half of your knowledge.

Welcome to a chaotic system!

A chaotic system is one where your success doesn't depend on how right you are. You can be wrong most of the time, and downright incompetent in this regard, and still progress. It's a bit like getting three out of 10 questions right on an exam and still receiving an A, with permission to move onto the next grade.

Thanks to us being conditioned in linear systems for so long, we cannot comprehend chaotic systems. Hence, we end up thinking the world is unfair. If some people are lucky, they eventually reach a stage where they recognize the folly of this kind of thinking and begin to understand how the world really works.

In trading terms, the markets being a prime example of a chaotic system has some very significant implications for the way you think about trading success.

Consider the scenario below: Which trader will make more money?

- Trader A who is right in their market predictions 30% of the time.
- Trader B who is right in their market predictions 90% of the time.

Take some time to think about this. If you're wondering what the correct answer is, I have to tell you that this is a trick question. I haven't given you enough information for you to be able to answer it...yet.

If you immediately said trader B is the one who will make more money and that trader A is a pretty abysmal trader, you've just defaulted to thinking linearly. The markets are chaotic. Being right is beside the point and it has no connection to how much money you'll make or how successful you'll be.

You need more information to be able to figure out how successful these traders are.

Win Rates

The 30% and 99% figures quoted in the above example are referred to as win rates or hit rates. Your hit rate is just one part of your trading success formula. This doesn't mean it's unimportant. It's just that it isn't the only metric in the picture that determines your success.

The other metric that is just as important is your average win and loss amount. In other words, how much do you win on average when you're right about the market's direction and how much do you lose on average when you're not?

Consider the following sequence of 10 trades for trailers A and B:

- Trader A - -1,-1,-1,-1,-1,-1,-1, 3, 3, 3
- Trader B - 1,1,1,1,1,1,1,1,1,-10

In these examples, I've assumed that each trader's win rate distributes itself perfectly over 10 trades. Trader A loses a dollar over seven trades but wins three dollars in the remaining three to preserve their 30% hit rate. Trader B wins a dollar nine times out of ten but then loses $10 in on trade. Their 90% hit rate is also preserved.

Again, who's the more successful trader? Clearly, A is the one who ends up making money. They make two dollars at the end of this sequence. Assuming they're risking one percent of their account and the one dollar represents one percent, they've just earned two percent over 10 trades.

If they place 10 trades like this over a month and assuming the distribution of wins and losses remains even on a monthly basis, trader A makes two percent every month. That's 24% per year assuming there's no compounding! That's a huge rate of return that any trader would kill to have. All this despite them being 'right' just 30% of the time.

Meanwhile, B doesn't even make money, let alone outperform A. They're right 90% of the time and still lose one percent over 10 trades. That's a loss of 12% per year! You'd be better off sticking your money in a savings account paying you 0.5% interest (if you're lucky) per year than give it to B. All of this despite B being 'right' 90% of the time.

Hopefully, you can see how overrated being right about the market's direction is when it comes to trading and chaotic systems in general. The number of right answers don't matter. You need to press home your advantage when you are right and minimize the damage when you're wrong. Success and being right don't have a one-to-one relationship, like they do in school when you're taking a test.

Keep in mind that it is fully possible for B to be profitable. All they need to do is lose less money on that solitary trade where they lose $10. If they lose just $5, then they're making a good amount of money.

My point is to show you that success exists on a large spectrum in the markets, instead of a tiny point as is the case with linear systems. In a linear system, in order to be successful you have to be right as much as possible. There is no other option you have.

In a chaotic system, such as the markets, there is a wide range of success. You can be right just 30% of the time and still make more money than the person who is right 90% of the time.

In this digital age a large number of venture capitalists have gained fame thanks to their investments. However, VCs have some of the highest failure rates in terms of their portfolios. For every successful startup they invest in, there are 10 more they misfired on. It doesn't matter, though. They make more money when they're right than they lose when they're wrong.

Remove the association between being right and making money in your mind. They're not directly connected. It's like saying all you need to successfully survive is air. This is technically true - but is it 'all' you need? You can have air but without water you'll die in a few days. You can have air and water but without food, you'll die in a few weeks. There's a lot more that goes into the equation of what you need.

Following this lesson, there are some significant thought processes or conclusions we can reach about the nature of trading.

Results Don't Matter

In the example with traders A and B, I've assumed that their hit rates will distribute themselves evenly over 10 trades. In the real world, there's no telling how the distribution will occur. They could lose 10 in a row or win 10 in a row. All that is certain is that over a large enough sample size, the distribution of wins and losses will come close to their hit rate.

Over 10 trades, the odds of them winning the number of trades their hit rates suggest is lower than it is over 1,000 trades. In turn, their odds over 1,000 trades are lower than they are over 10,000 trades and so on.

The point here is that as long as the trader keeps repeating their successful process, over time their wins and losses will equal their hit rate. Therefore, over a large enough sample size, they will make money.

If they lose 10 trades now, at some point their hit rate will reassert itself, and they will end up making money. If they know that they'll make money over the long term, should they even care about the result of a solitary trade? The answer is no, they shouldn't.

After all, how does a win or loss on a single trade change anything. The win that occurs now will be substituted by losses at some point. The loss that occurs now will be offset by some combination of wins. All that matters is that the trader keeps doing the things that bring them their hit rate and their average win and loss size.

I must mention that you should be aware of falling into the gambler's fallacy. If a trader loses 10 trades in a row and has a 40% hit rate, this doesn't mean they're statistically likely to win the majority of their next 10. They could still lose the next 10 since results are random.

It's like saying that, just because red has come up 10 times in a row on the roulette table, black is sure to come up the 11th time. That's not how it works. Remember that chaotic systems are irrational. They can produce results that make no sense.

Instead, you need to think in terms of odds. You keep trading your system over and over and maintain good risk management principles (that you'll learn about in this chapter) and you'll make money. You might not make money over a month. You might not even make money over a year.

However, the longer you apply successful principles, the better your odds are of making money over the long term. The problem arises when you put too much pressure on yourself and think that individual results are important. They simply aren't.

Numbers Matter

If the odds of hitting your hit rate improve with the number of trades you take, it follows that, in order to be successful, you need to trade your system as much as possible. This means once you've landed upon a successful system, your task is to replicate that system across as many instruments and markets as possible.

This will increase the number of trades you take and will increase your potential profits as well. After all, it's just a matter of odds playing themselves out. Having said that, don't be in a rush to go ahead and trade as many instruments as possible. You need to work your way up to expanding your portfolio.

It's best to begin with a solitary instrument and run it through the framework that I'll discuss in the seven steps in the next chapter. Once you've done this, you can add more instruments and gradually scale your trading operations. Rushing in and trading everything in sight is what novices do.

Don't be a novice.

Consistency

Another key principle that arises from the example of traders A and B is that of consistency. Let's say A messes around with the amount of money they lose when they're wrong. Instead of this being -1, let's say they lose -1 on some trades and -3 on others.

This means their average loss fluctuates with every trade and, if their hit rate remains the same, it has the potential to move them out of the profit zone. If a trader has a hit rate of 30%, they need to maintain an average win to loss ratio of at least 2.5 to break even.

The amount they win needs to be 2.5 times the amount they lose when they're incorrect. If B is inconsistent in exiting losing trades and becomes an inadvertent investor whenever the trade goes against them, they're going to increase their average loss size and reduce the win to loss ratio.

The win to loss ratio is also called the reward to risk ratio. Your average loss should be the maximum amount of risk you face in a trade. It should be the amount you lose if you're incorrect about the market's direction.

This means your position sizes need to be tailored to your risk. In the stock market it's pretty easy to calculate this. You divide the average loss you desire (your risk per trade) by the distance between your entry and stop loss. This is your position size. In FX, it's best to use a calculator, thanks to the variations that currencies bring.

Since your stop loss distance will vary depending on the existence of sr nearby, your position sizes will fluctuate. What will not fluctuate is your risk per trade. Your rewards need to be at a multiple that allows you to make a profit based on your hit rate or more than this.

This is how you determine your exit points as well. For example, a trader with a 30% hit rate needs to have a reward to risk ratio of 2.5R. R is the amount you'll lose on average and is your risk per trade.

Start focusing on R instead of win and loss amounts. Keep it consistent and you'll make the risk math work for you.

Risk Per Trade

How should you arrive at an appropriate risk per trade? When you're starting out, this is the only value you can fix definitively. After all, you can ballpark an average exit multiple but you can't predict what your hit rate will be. It all begins with fixing an appropriate R amount.

There are two schools of thought to doing this. The first is to fix R as a particular numerical amount and the second is the fix R as a percentage of your capital. The second method is unequivocally better. This is because R, as a fixed percentage, gives you greater control over your risk math and allows you to scale your operations better.

Imagine you adopt a fixed amount model and fix an arbitrary number, say $500, as being your risk per trade. Let's say you win three in a row and make 2R on each trade. You've just made $3,000. Will you keep your R fixed at $500? Or will you increase it?

Let's say you increase it to $700. Now, let's say you lose 4 in a row for a total loss of $2,800. You've just come right back to your starting point.

This kind of volatility always occurs with unsuccessful traders; it's because they keep switching their R amounts. You've already seen how consistency is important. If you kept your R fixed at $500 throughout, you would have lost less money. However, you would have made far less money as well as a percentage of your account.

As your account grows in size, your risk per trade is a smaller percentage of your account. Thus, your gains will be smaller, as well, since your wins are a multiple of R. In effect, you'll wish that your account was smaller. That way, you could earn a bigger return on your capital!

Under a fixed percentage model, there's no question beforehand about how much you need to risk. Every trade will have a different risk amount but your percentage returns will remain consistent. What's more, if you happen to hit a losing streak, your risk amounts will decrease because your percentage risk remains the same.

Therefore, your loss curve will grow shallow. On the flip side, if you hit a win streak then your win curve accelerates because you're risking a large amount as your account grows in size.

The final argument in favor of a fixed percentage model is the concept of risk of ruin (Chen, 2019). This is a statistical concept that I'm not going to spend too much time discussing, because it's irrelevant. Your risk of ruin is the probability of you losing all of your money. If this is fixed at zero, and if you keep everything else consistent, you cannot lose your capital ever. It's a mathematical certainty.

Risk of ruin cannot be calculated using a fixed amount model. You need to use a fixed percent model to be able to figure out what your risk of ruin is.

Behavior

A part of trading that most people ignore is their own mindset when it comes to money. The field of behavioral economics has grown immensely over the past few decades. This field of study seeks to measure and observe how human beings perceive risk. The detailed analysis you've read in this chapter of chaotic versus linear systems stems from behavioral economics papers.

While this is an immensely theoretical field and has many uses, from a trading perspective you need to understand that monitoring your psyche is just as important as monitoring the effectiveness of your technical strategy.

Since trading is such a subjective pursuit, you need to apply consistency to everything you do. If your mindset is affected, your results will be as well. For example, if you're disturbed about something in your personal life, don't trade. Your brain needs to work at peak capacity and if you're disturbed or are somehow not on an even keel, you cannot hope to make impartial decisions.

Examining your beliefs about money is crucial for this. All beliefs can be overcome with awareness. None of us grew up in perfect households and as a result, all of us possess harmful beliefs. Some of us believe we're destined to be poor while others believe that money is evil.

It's safe to say that if you pit trading against such beliefs, there are going to be huge emotional upheavals in your life. It isn't important to figure out what caused the negative belief. Awareness and replacing that belief with new thoughts is more critical for your success.

Behavioral economics also teaches us that we are far more risk averse than the degree with which we desire gains. In other words we value gains and losses differently (Chen, 2019).

Consider the following situation. You're presented with an investment opportunity. These are the facts. The investment has averaged the following returns over 10 years:

- 10%
- 10%
- 10%
- 11%
- 15%
- 2%
- 3%
- 5%
- 16%
- 4%

The average investment performance over the 10-year period is 8.5%. Over the preceding three-year period, it is 8.3% which is less than the average.

Let's say two people present this same opportunity in the following ways:

- One person tells you that the average return of this opportunity is 8.5% and it has recently returned as high as 16%, which is a record.
- The other tells you that the average return of this investment is 8.5% but it has declined over the last three years, on average.

Which one sounds more desirable to you? All of us would choose the first statement. However, both are describing the same situation. The negativity bias in our brains causes us to frame the first statement as being more desirable. To be successful at trading, you have to remember that your negativity bias will cause you to focus a lot more on your losses than on your wins.

Losing streaks will occur and you'll begin to think your system is rubbish. This is why the principle I highlighted previously, of realizing that individual results don't matter in the least, is so important. It helps you overcome your negativity bias or keep it at bay at the very least.

This will get you to focus on the really important stuff. Like being consistent in your trading practice in order to make money.

Chapter 9:

Seven Steps to Successful Trading

You've learned a lot of information throughout this book. Now, it's time to put it all together into an easily adoptable framework. The seven steps here will help you approach your trading in a systematic manner and will allow you to scale your trading operations in an intelligent manner as well.

Resist the temptation to breeze through or skip some steps. All of them are here for a reason.

Step One - Determine Your Capital

This is a step that most traders skip. In order to be successful at trading you need to risk capital that you can fully afford to lose. So, don't quit your day job just yet. You should have enough money set aside for at least three months' worth of living expenses as well as any other foreseeable expenses.

Never put yourself in a position where you 'have' to make money from the market. It is unpredictable and chaotic. Being a servant to it will only throw your brain off balance and will cause you to make poor decisions.

You'll also need to figure out which market you wish to operate in at this time. As you've already learned, operating successfully in stocks requires you to possess at least $25,000 in capital. It's best to begin with FX if you don't have access to this amount of money.

Step Two - Simulation

Once you've figured out how much capital you can raise, your next step should be to begin developing your trading strategy. This is the longest step of them all and you'll be spending most of your time here, even when you're trading live.

In order to develop your strategy, you need to invest in a software that allows you to replay and simulate prior market data. Regarding the FX market, Forextester is a great product. For the stock market you can use NinjaTrader. This will cost you money but consider it an investment.

It'll pay itself many times over once you develop a great strategy. You should begin by learning the basics as described in this book. Don't worry about placing trades. Simply focus on identifying the different kinds of ranges that exist and the trends that accompany them.

Cycle through time frames to see how charts change. A small range in one time frame might be a large one in another that signals a potential trend change on that smaller time frame. Take the time to place your trades to see what works best for you. Don't bother with live markets at this point.

Once you've fixed a strategy in place, it's time to test it. Place 1,000 simulated trades on your software. This might sound like a lot but remember that you can speed up the rate at which bars move in the software. If you can place 25 trades every day, it'll take you a little over a month to place these trades.

If you think you can't be bothered with 1,000 and that 100 sounds like a better number, remember that your aim is to be a professional. Bank traders do not sniff real money until they've proved themselves profitable over 1,000+ trades in their simulation platforms. You ought to approach it in the same way.

Step Three - Analyze and Fix

1,000 trades is going to give you a ton of data and it'll also help embed your strategy into your mind completely. By the end of this exercise, you'll likely have no doubts about how your strategy works. You might have even tweaked it.

It's important to place these many trades since you need to figure out the optimal risk math for your strategy. All simulation software helps you monitor these metrics through reports so this is just a matter of clicking a button.

Check to see if your strategy is profitable. If it is, is there a way for you to increase your reward to risk ratio? Doing this will impact your hit rate as well. Review your trades to quickly see whether there were any additional profits you could have made.

You should gather the following metrics:

- Hit rate
- Average win to average loss ratio
- Max drawdown (the difference between your highest account balance peak and the immediate trough that followed)
- Recovery time (the time it took you to make a new equity high from the trough of the max drawdown)

Once you've figured out your metrics, it's time to move on to the next step.

Step Four - Determine Risk

This step is where you'll fix your risk per trade. When you start out, you should not be risking more than 0.5% of your account. Some sources recommend two percent but this is a huge amount of risk for a beginner to assume. If you run into a losing streak of 10 trades, you'll lose 20% of your capital!

Risking just 0.5% helps you keep your emotions in check and you'll be able to adopt the attitude of not caring about individual results far better.

Next, you'll also need to fix your drawdown limits. Putting these limits in place will prevent you from losing too much capital. You need to have session, weekly and monthly limits.

As a rule of thumb, your session drawdown limit should be three losing trades in a row when starting out, a limit of two percent of your account as a weekly limit and four percent as your monthly limit.

Step Five - Demo

You're not ready to trade live just yet! It's time to now demo trade your strategy. FX brokers routinely provide demo accounts to their clients. If you're in the stock market, you'll need to trade via Ninjatrader through their daily market replay function.

Treat this time as if you're trading in the market for real. Risk the right amounts and be consistent with your actions. Your objective is to demo trade for a period of six months and to make money by the end of it as a whole.

You can lose money in some months or even in five months in a row. What's important is that you make money at the end of a rolling six-month period while following your risk drawdown limits. Do not move to the next step unless this is in place! Follow all of your risk parameters and at the end of the six-month period, you'll find that you'll make money.

Step Six - Live Trading

With all of this prep work behind you, it's now time to trade live money. Choose your broker wisely and begin trading live. You'll have placed well over 1,000 trades by now and it should feel automatic to you. You'll have also made money on paper so you should have confidence in your abilities.

When trading live, it's important to journal all of your trades. Note down the entry and exit points as well as the reasons for entry and exit. Take screenshots of your entry and exits. Also maintain a record of your mental state before, during and after your trades.

Review your trades on a weekly basis and pinpoint any areas that need fixing or enhancement. Keep working on improving your system by practicing your skills on simulation platforms.

Step Seven - Scale

You can begin step seven concurrently with step five. In order to scale your trading, you'll need to repeat this process with every other new instrument you choose to add to your portfolio. Run it through the sme framework. Obviously, keep the risk per trade consistent across all instruments in your portfolio.

You want the math to be consistent so don't risk 0.5% in one instrument and 0.25% in another. Run 1,000 simulated trades, demo trade the instrument for six months and bring it live after this time. You can work on adding more than one instrument at a time after you've successfully gone live with the first instrument. Begin with one and then add two or three the next time around so that you scale in a sensible manner.

Conclusion

So, there you have it! Seven steps to trading success that tie together everything you've learned in this book. Build your trading system from the ground up by analyzing the range/trend characteristics of the market. You can add indicators to this if you wish but remember to keep them only as supplements to your system.

Trading is a journey and while the money on offer is huge, remember that you need to work for it in order to get there. Many traders start off well but get overconfident and risk far too much due to greed. Resist the temptation to do this. Simply keep doing whatever makes you money.

If this means trading just one timeframe, so be it. You might be tempted to move into day trading and this is great. However, build your swing trading skills first before moving down to lower time frames. This way you'll be expanding with a stable base already setup.

It's easy to fall into the trap of wanting to make quick and easy money. Such schemes rarely bear fruit. Trading will reward patience and persistence not greed. Make sure you execute each and every step perfectly and you'll be rewarded before you know it.

Review the material in the risk management chapter constantly. It will take you time to internalize all of this information. All of us have been taught to think in a certain manner and the material in that chapter is contrarian advice. As such, it will take you time to understand all the implications thinking like that brings.

As I close out this book, I'd like to thank you for taking the positive step towards a better life that trading can give you. There's no doubt that it is a great endeavor. But you'll have to put in the work to get there. I wish you all the luck and profits in the world!

Do let me know what you think of this book by leaving me a review. Let me know what you learned and also what you felt changed your opinion of certain things. I'd love to hear from you!

Until then, happy trading!

References

Chen, J. (2019). Prospect Theory. Retrieved 7 June
      2020, from
      https://www.investopedia.com/terms/p/prosp
      ecttheory.asp

Chen, J. (2019). Risk of Ruin. Retrieved 7 June 2020,
      from
      https://www.investopedia.com/terms/r/risk-
      of-ruin.asp

Kuepper, J. (2020). Call Option. Retrieved 7 June 2020,
      from
      https://www.investopedia.com/terms/c/callop
      tion.asp

Pattern Day Trader. (2020). Retrieved 7 June 2020,
      from https://www.sec.gov/fast-
      answers/answerspatterndaytraderhtm.html#:~:t
      ext=FINRA%20rules%20define%20a%20%E2
      %80%9Cpattern,same%20five%20business%20
      day%20period

Rodriguez, D. (2017). Why Do Many Forex Traders
      Lose Money? Here is the Number 1 Mistake.
      Retrieved 7 June 2020, from
      https://www.dailyfx.com/forex/fundamental/a

rticle/special_report/2015/06/25/what-is-the-
number-one-mistake-forex-traders-make.html

Segal, T. (2017). Forex Folk: Who Trades Currency and
Why. Retrieved 7 June 2020, from
https://www.investopedia.com/articles/forex/
11/who-trades-forex-and-
why.asp#:~:text=The%20foreign%20exchange
%20or%20forex,FX%20and%20OTC%20deriv
atives%20markets

Chart images sourced from tradingview.com

Images sourced from pixabay.com